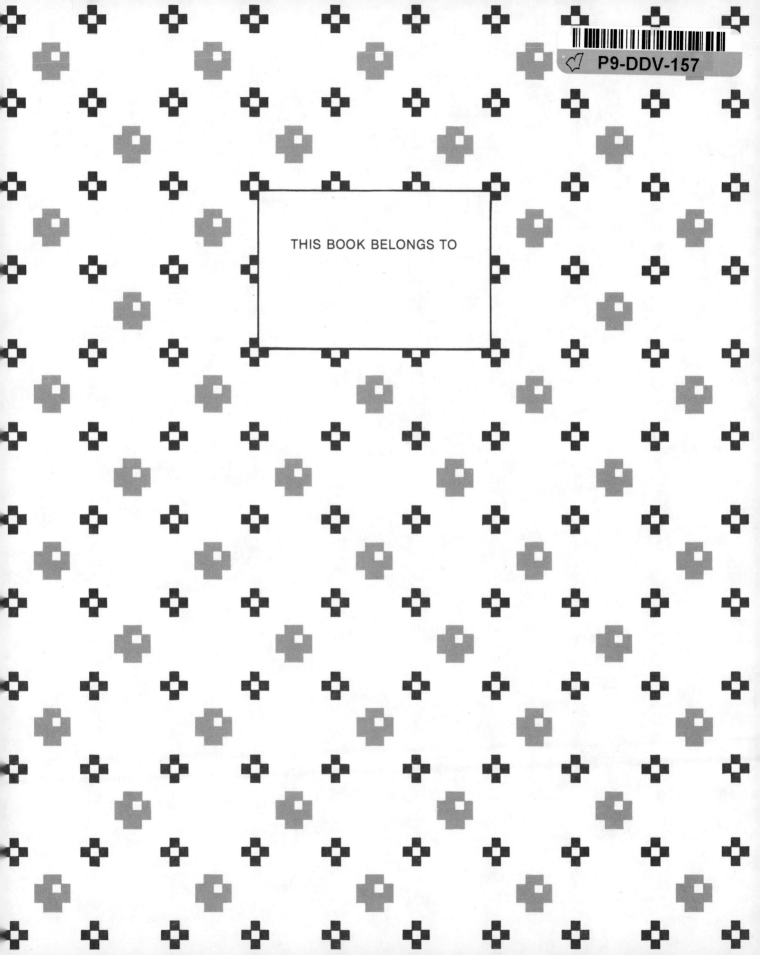

THIS BOOK BELONGS TO

GIFTS OF NATURE
By Marie Barber

An American Sampler

GIFTS OF NATURE
By Marie Barber

An American Sampler

Meredith® Press

New York, New York

Meredith® Press is an imprint of Meredith® Books:
President, Book Group: Joseph J. Ward
Vice-President, Editorial Director: Elizabeth P. Rice
For Meredith® Press
Executive Editor: Maryanne Bannon
Senior Editor: Carol Spier
Associate Editor: Ruth Weadock
Production Manager: Bill Rose

For Chapelle Limited
Owner: Jo Packham
Staff: Sandra Anderson, Malissa Boatwright,
Trice Boerens, Rebecca Christensen, Holly Fuller,
Cherie Hanson, Holly Hollingsworth,
Susan Jorgensen, Susan Laws, Lorin May,
Tammy Perkins, Jamie C. Pierce, Leslie Ridenour,
Amy Vineyard, Nancy Whitley, and Lorrie Young

Photographer: Ryne Hazen
Framing by: Artist's Touch

The photographs in this book were taken at the
home of Jo Packham.

ISBN: 0-696-20036-8
Library of Congress Catalog Card Number: 94-077307
First Printing 1994
Published by Meredith Press

Distributed by Meredith Corporation, Des Moines, IA.

10 9 8 7 6 5 4 3 2 1

All rights reserved.

Printed in the United States of America.

Dear Crafter,

One of the greatest inspirations for stitching is the living beauty of Nature herself: The resplendent orchard in spring, the glorious bouquets of summer, the ripe bounty of the fall harvest—these are some of the sublime visions that the artist, Marie Barber, has captured in *An American Sampler: Gifts of Nature.*

As the seventh annual volume in our series of distinctive cross-stitch books, *Gifts of Nature* is a special pleasure to bring to our readers, whether those familiar with or just discovering these exquisite titles.

To complement each beautiful design, we have presented the projects—which range from grand, gorgeous framed works to petite, pretty "weekenders"—in captivating photographs, with clear directions and easy-to-read charts. There's even a section on stitching basics—a primer for beginners or "refresher" for the more experienced.

Nature's gifts of blue skies and floral vistas are perhaps the most wondrous of all. We hope that you will find just a hint of Her breathtaking splendor in the samplers and gifts you create from these pages.

Enjoy,

Ruth A. Weadock

Ruth Weadock
Associate Editor

All of us at Meredith® Press are dedicated to offering you, our customer, the best books we can create. We are particularly concerned that all of the instructions for making projects are clear and accurate. Please address your correspondence to Customer Service Department, Meredith® Press, 150 East 52nd Street, New York, NY 10022 or call 1-800-678-8091.

CONTENTS

**If you truly
love Nature, you
will find
beauty everywhere.**

–Vincent Van Gogh

Stitch Count: 160 x 230

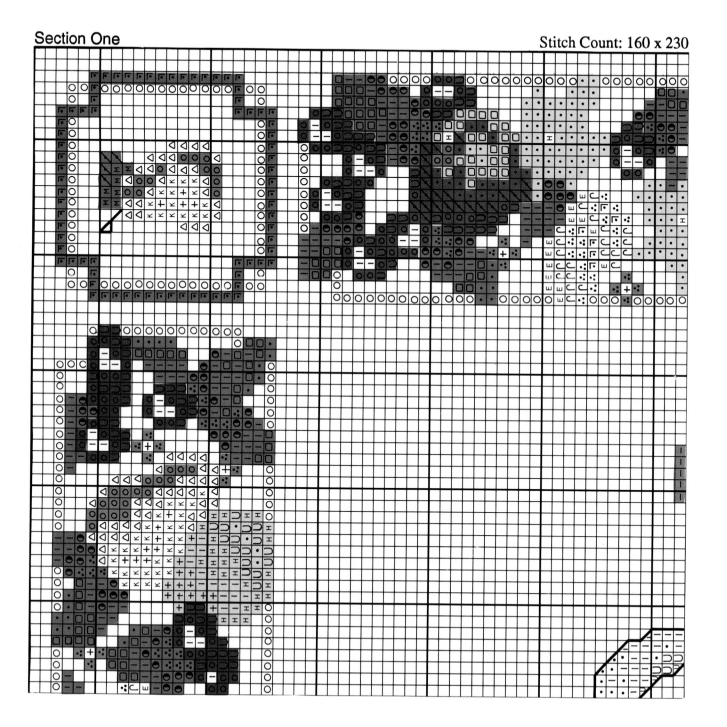

Section Two

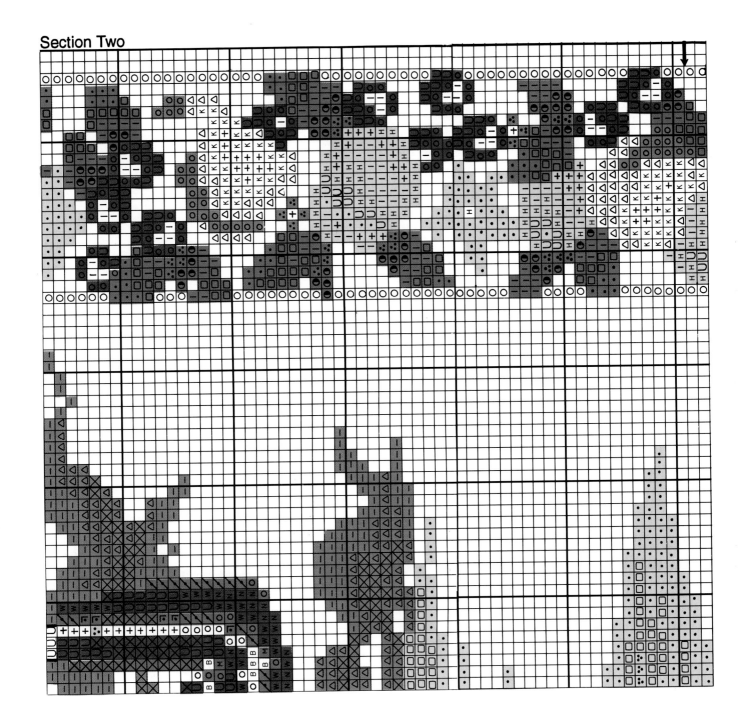

Section Three

10

Section Four

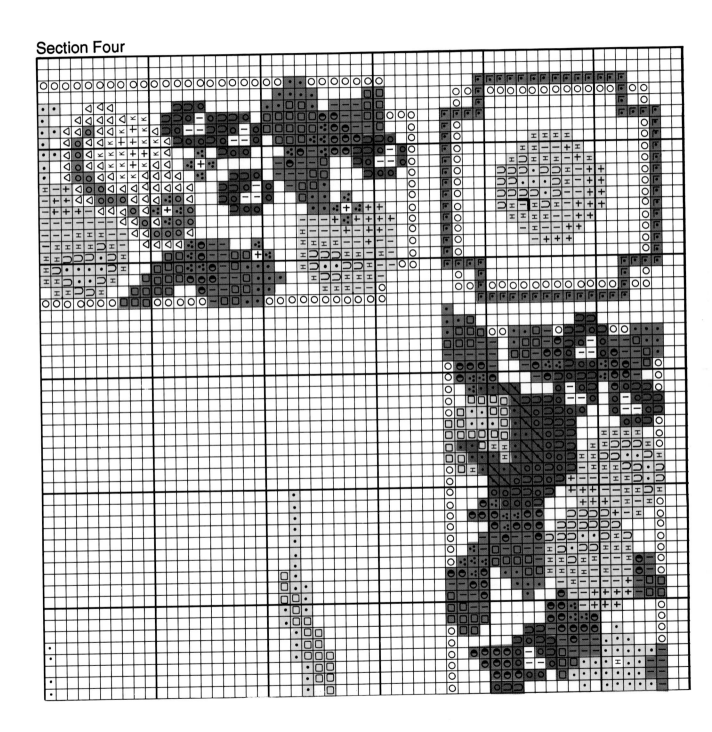

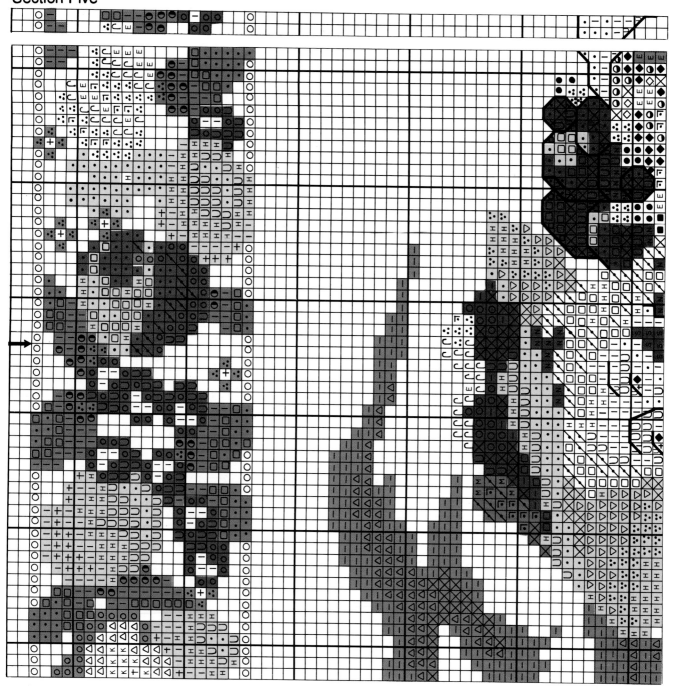

Section Six

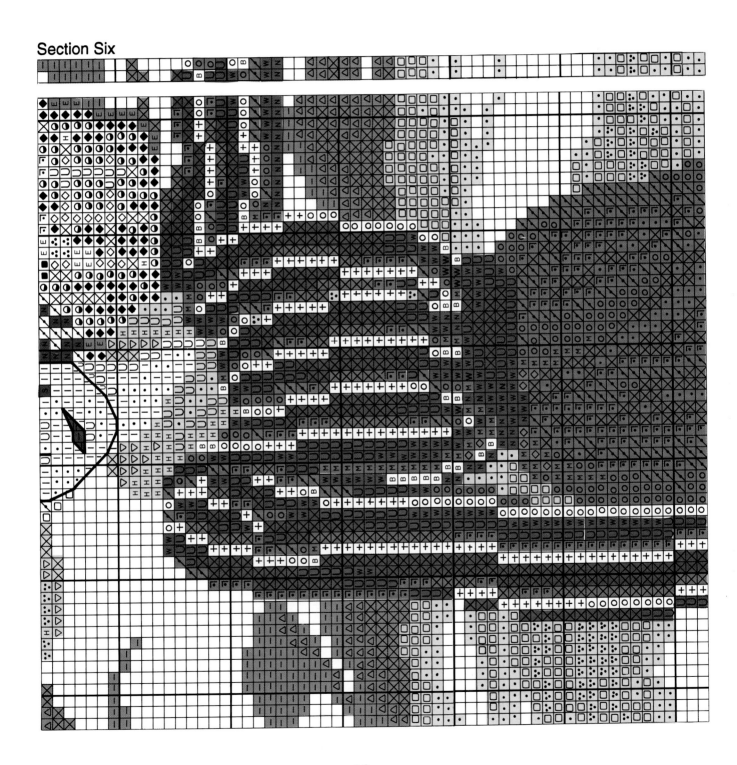

Section Seven

Section Eight

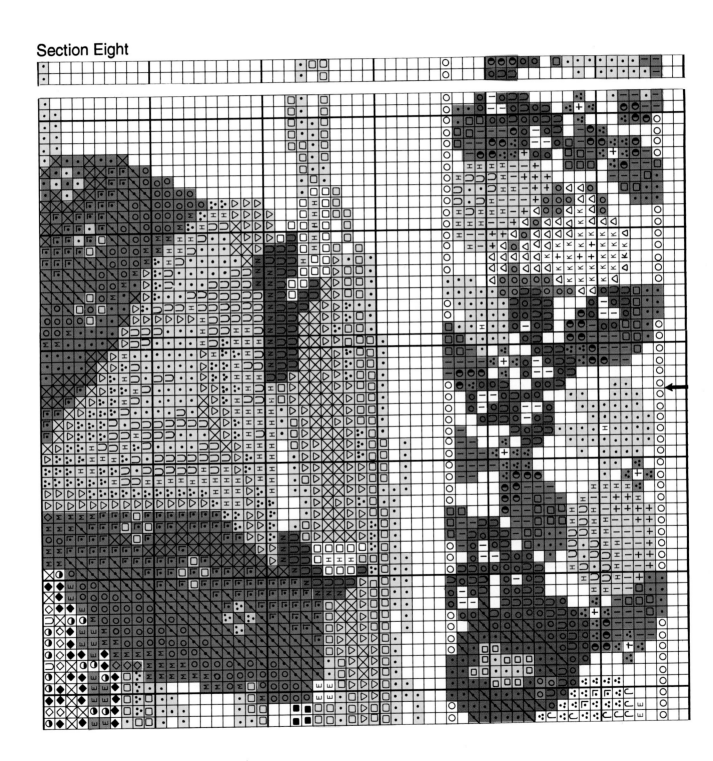

Section Nine

Section Ten

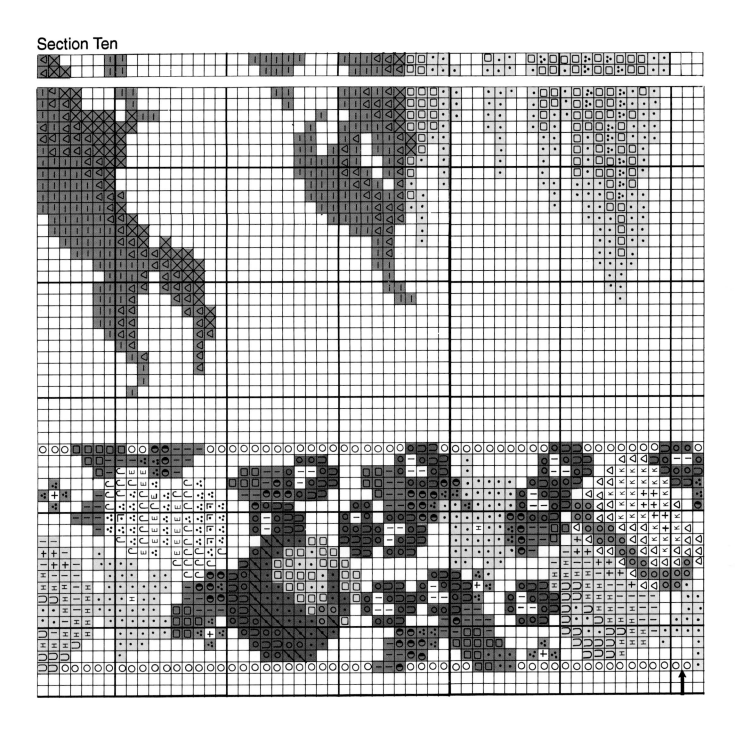

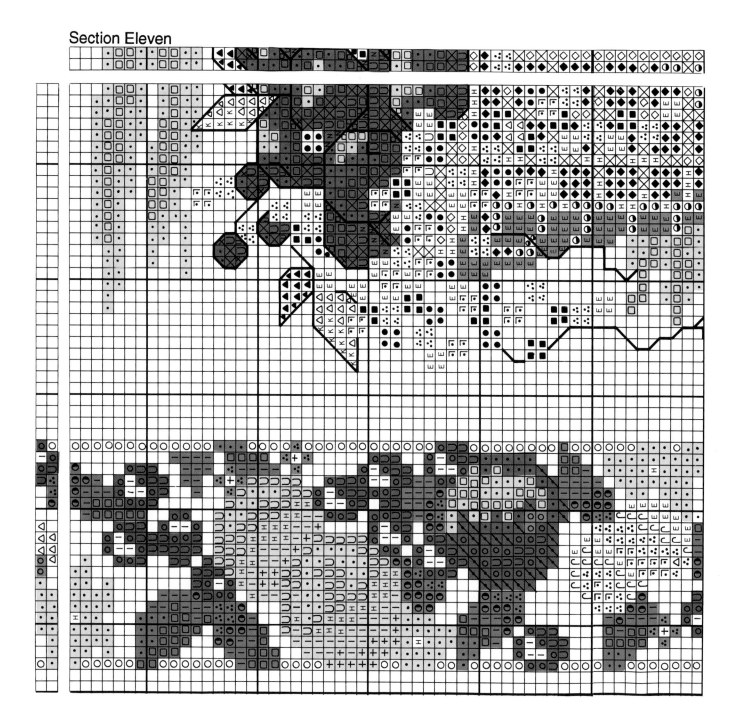

Section Twelve

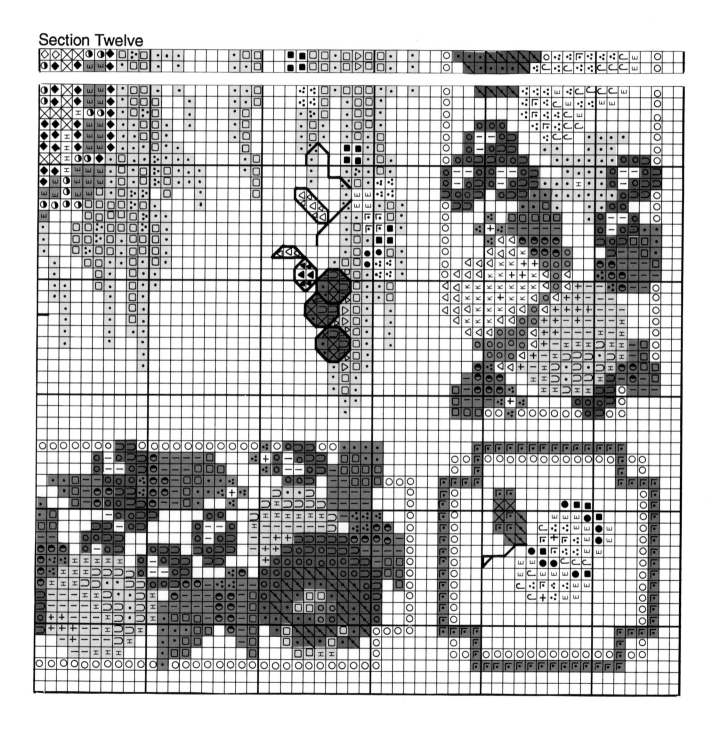

Fruit Maiden

Stitched on antique white Jobelan 28 over two threads, the finished design size is 11½" x 16½". The fabric was cut 18" x 23". See diagram below for graph page placement. Frame piece as desired.

FABRICS	DESIGN SIZES
Aida 11	14½" x 20⅞"
Aida 14	11⅜" x 16⅜"
Aida 18	8⅞" x 12¾"
Hardanger 22	7¼" x 10½"

Stitch Count: 160 x 230

Top of Design

Section One (page 8)	Section Two (page 9)	Section Three (page 10)	Section Four (page 11)
Section Five (page 12)	Section Six (page 13)	Section Seven (page 14)	Section Eight (page 15)
Section Nine (page 16)	Section Ten (page 17)	Section Eleven (page 18)	Section Twelve (page 19)

Diagram

Anchor **DMC (used for sample)**

Step 1: Cross-stitch (2 strands)

Anchor	Symbol		DMC	Color
1	+	◹		White
300	•		745	Yellow-lt. pale
891	□	◹	676	Old Gold-lt.
890	∴		729	Old Gold-med.
307	I		977	Golden Brown-lt.
380	◆	◢	839	Beige Brown-dk.
265	K	◹	3348	Yellow Green-lt.
266	△	◹	3347	Yellow Green-med.
268	▲	◹	3345	Hunter Green-dk.
214	✕		368	Pistachio Green-lt.
215	◙		320	Pistachio Green-med.
216	◸	◹	367	Pistachio Green-dk.
879	M		890	Pistachio Green-ultra dk.
213	•		504	Blue Green-lt.
875	◘		503	Blue Green-med.
878	∷		501	Blue Green-dk.
900	○		3024	Brown Gray-vy. lt.
8581	B		647	Beaver Gray-med.
5975	H		356	Terra Cotta-med.

Anchor	Symbol		DMC	Color
341	◹		3777	Terra Cotta-vy. dk.
880	•	◹	948	Peach-vy. lt.
933	I	◹	3774	Peach Pecan-med.
4146	U	◹	950	Peach Pecan-dk.
882	✕		407	Pecan
108	◙		211	Lavender-lt.
105	∴		209	Lavender-dk.
99	E		552	Violet-dk.
101	●		550	Violet-vy. dk.
158	△		775	Baby Blue-vy. lt.
159	✕		3325	Baby Blue-lt.
121	∴		793	Cornflower Blue-med.
9	◤	◹	760	Salmon
10	◎		3328	Salmon-dk.
11	✕	◢	350	Coral-med.
19	U	◹	817	Coral Red-vy. dk.
43	N	◹	815	Garnet-med.
876	I		502	Blue Green

21

Step 2: Blended Cross-stitch (1 strand each)

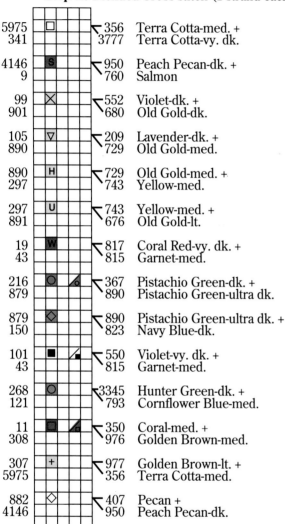

5975 / 341	□	356 / 3777 — Terra Cotta-med. + Terra Cotta-vy. dk.
4146 / 9	S	950 / 760 — Peach Pecan-dk. + Salmon
99 / 901	✕	552 / 680 — Violet-dk. + Old Gold-dk.
105 / 890	▽	209 / 729 — Lavender-dk. + Old Gold-med.
890 / 297	H	729 / 743 — Old Gold-med. + Yellow-med.
297 / 891	U	743 / 676 — Yellow-med. + Old Gold-lt.
19 / 43	W	817 / 815 — Coral Red-vy. dk. + Garnet-med.
216 / 879	◉	367 / 890 — Pistachio Green-dk. + Pistachio Green-ultra dk.
879 / 150	◇	890 / 823 — Pistachio Green-ultra dk. + Navy Blue-dk.
101 / 43	■	550 / 815 — Violet-vy. dk. + Garnet-med.
268 / 121	◉	3345 / 793 — Hunter Green-dk. + Cornflower Blue-med.
11 / 308	▣	350 / 976 — Coral-med. + Golden Brown-med.
307 / 5975	+	977 / 356 — Golden Brown-lt. + Terra Cotta-med.
882 / 4146	◇	407 / 950 — Pecan + Peach Pecan-dk.

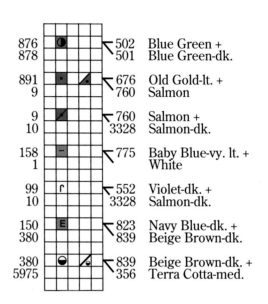

876 / 878	◐	502 / 501 — Blue Green + Blue Green-dk.
891 / 9	▪	676 / 760 — Old Gold-lt. + Salmon
9 / 10	◢	760 / 3328 — Salmon + Salmon-dk.
158 / 1	−	775 — Baby Blue-vy. lt. + White
99 / 10	⌐	552 / 3328 — Violet-dk. + Salmon-dk.
150 / 380	E	823 / 839 — Navy Blue-dk. + Beige Brown-dk.
380 / 5975	◑	839 / 356 — Beige Brown-dk. + Terra Cotta-med.

Step 3: Backstitch (1 strand)

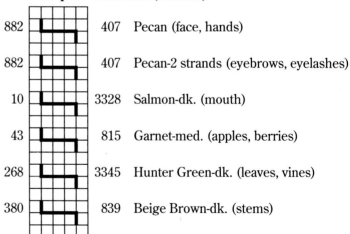

882		407 — Pecan (face, hands)
882		407 — Pecan-2 strands (eyebrows, eyelashes)
10		3328 — Salmon-dk. (mouth)
43		815 — Garnet-med. (apples, berries)
268		3345 — Hunter Green-dk. (leaves, vines)
380		839 — Beige Brown-dk. (stems)

23

Coaster

Stitched on moss green Murano 30 over two threads, the finished design size is 1⅜" x 1⅜" for each motif. The fabric was cut 9" x 9". The designs are the corner fruit motifs of the large framed piece and are taken from the graphs on pages 8, 11, 16, and 19. Begin stitching each design 2" from each corner. Trim stitched design piece to 5½" square. Place over same size batting and backing fabric and bind edges with 1½" x 23" piece of desired bias fabric.

FABRICS	DESIGN SIZES
Aida 11	6⅛" x 6⅛"
Aida 14	4⅞" x 4⅞"
Aida 18	3¾" x 3¾"
Hardanger 22	3⅛" x 3⅛"

Towel

Stitched on a 14-count towel over two threads, the finished design size is 8⅜" x 1⅜". The design is the bottom fruit border of the large framed piece and is taken from the graphs on pages 11, 15, and 19. Add ribbon or trim as desired. See page 143 for supplier.

FABRICS	DESIGN SIZES
Aida 11	10¾" x 1⅞"
Aida 14	8⅜" x 1⅜"
Aida 18	6½" x 1⅛"
Hardanger 22	5⅜" x ⅞"

Basket Buttons

Stitched on moss green Murano 30 over two threads, the finished design size is 1⅜" x 1⅜" for each button. The fabric was cut 6" x 6". The designs are the corner motifs of the large framed piece and are taken from the graphs on pages 8, 11, 16, and 19. Cover purchased 1½" button forms with stitched designs. Pleat 3"-wide band of fabric as shown, sew on buttons, and attach to basket.

FABRICS	DESIGN SIZES
Aida 11	1⅞" x 1⅞"
Aida 14	1⅜" x 1⅜"
Aida 18	1⅛" x 1⅛"
Hardanger 22	⅞" x ⅞"

**Apprentice yourself
to Nature. Not a day
will pass without her
opening a new and
wondrous world to
learn from and enjoy.**

–Richard W. Langer

Section One   Stitch Count: 154 x 227

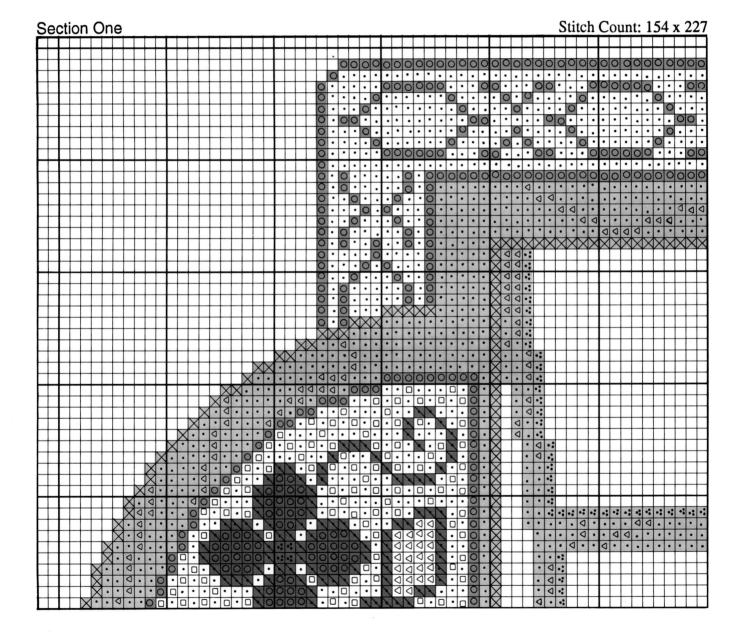

Section Two

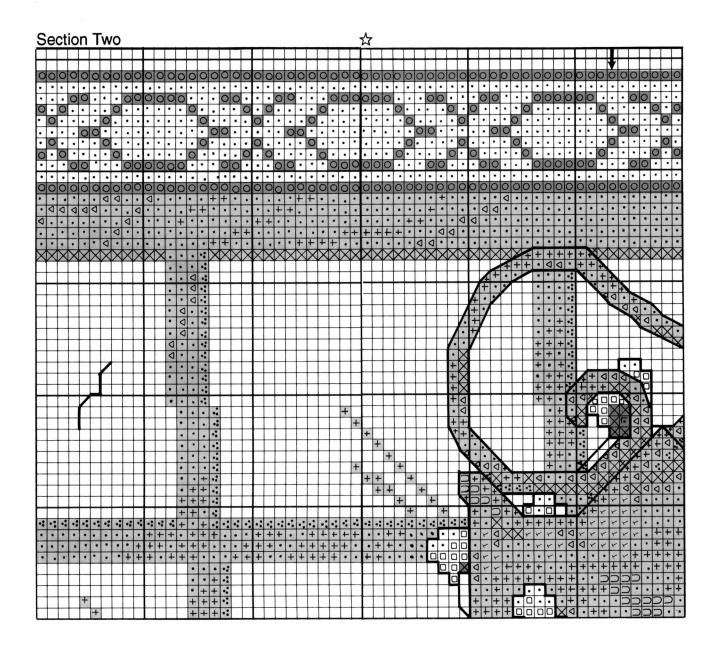

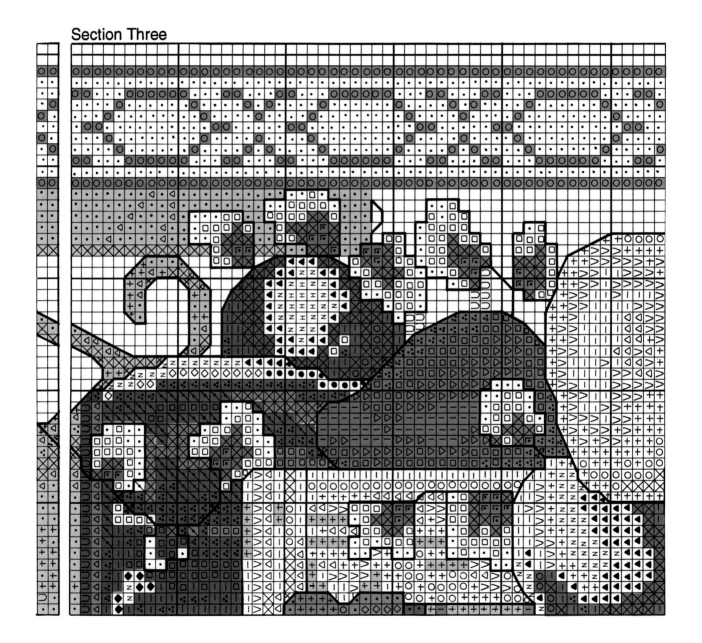

30

Section Four

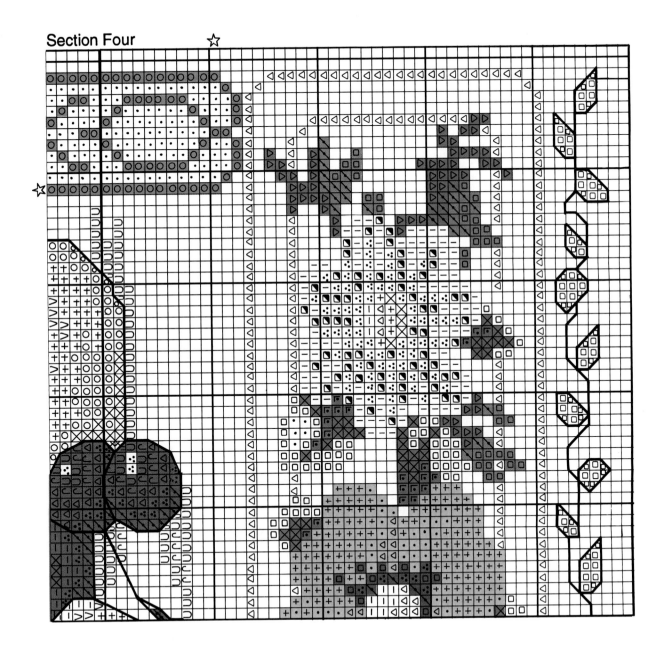

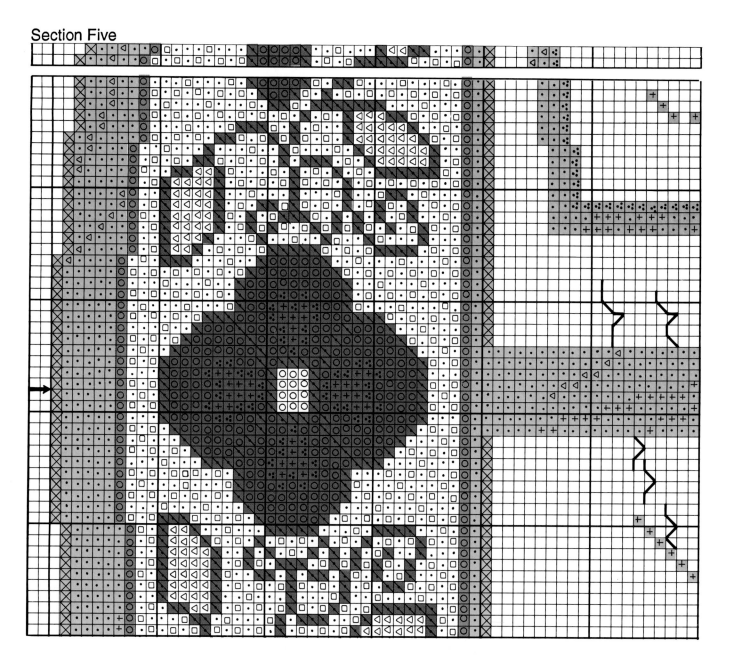

Section Six

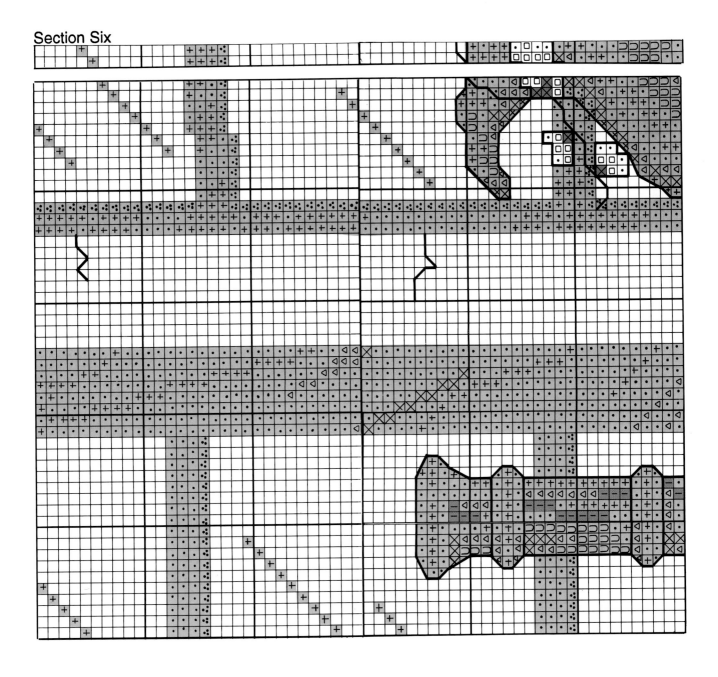

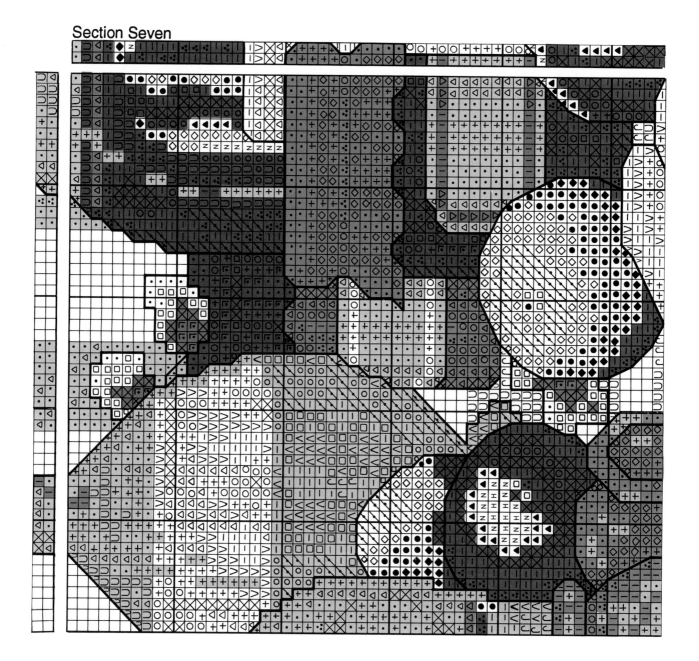

34

Section Eight

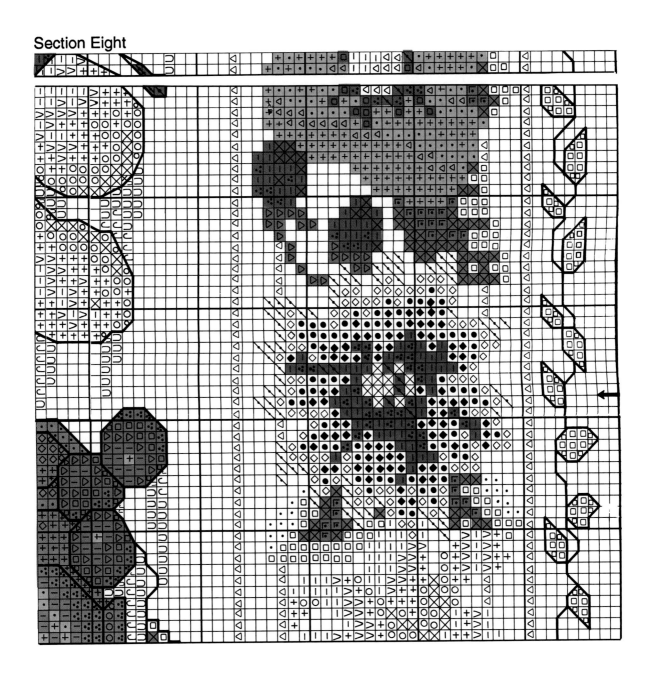

Section Nine

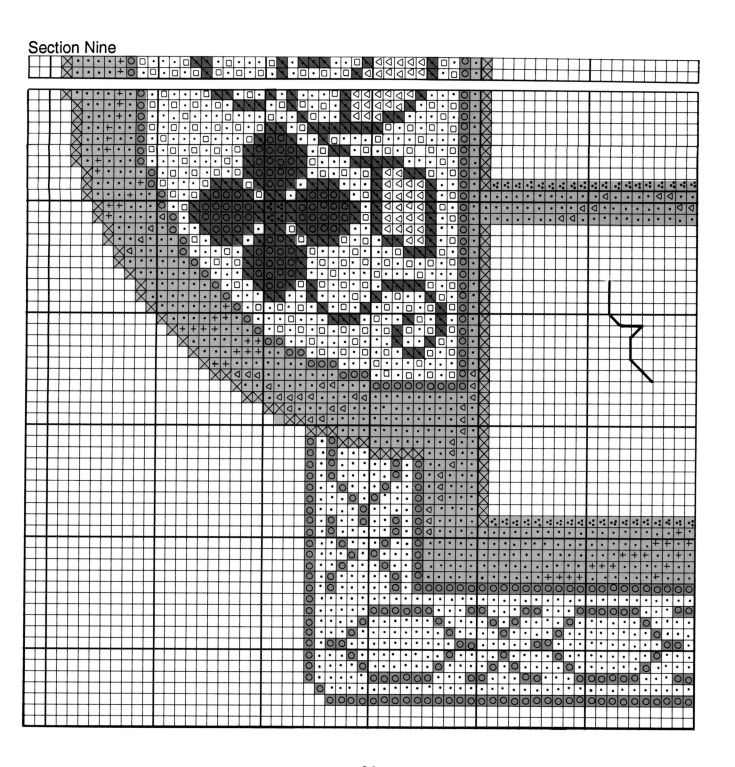

Section Ten

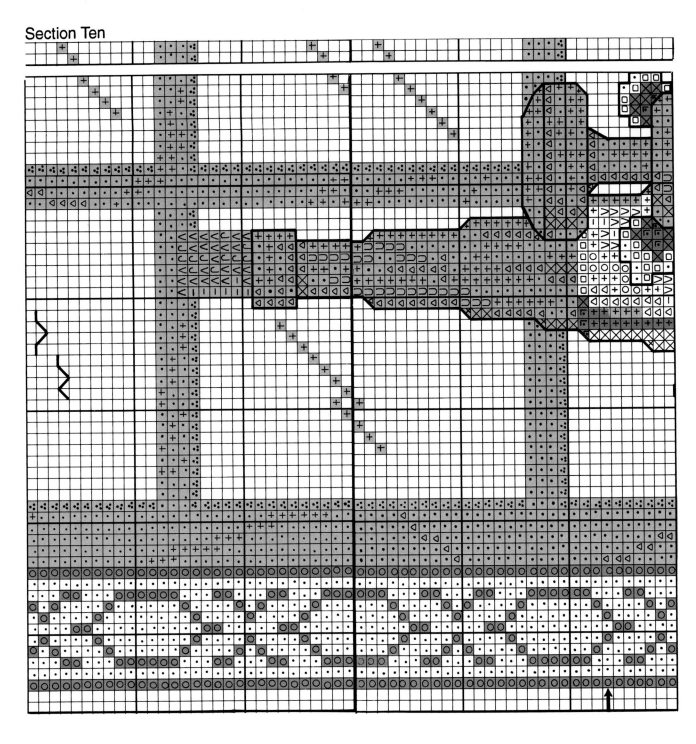

Section Eleven

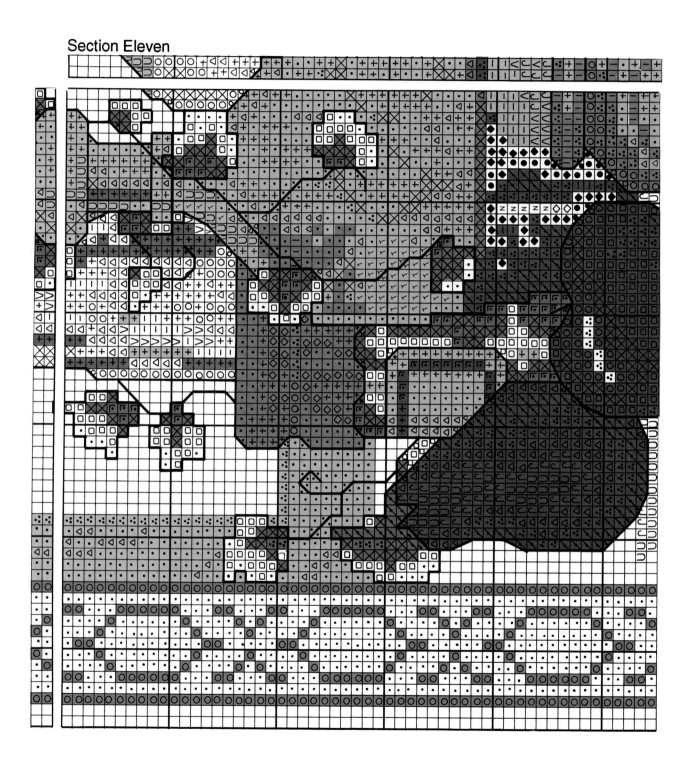

Section Twelve

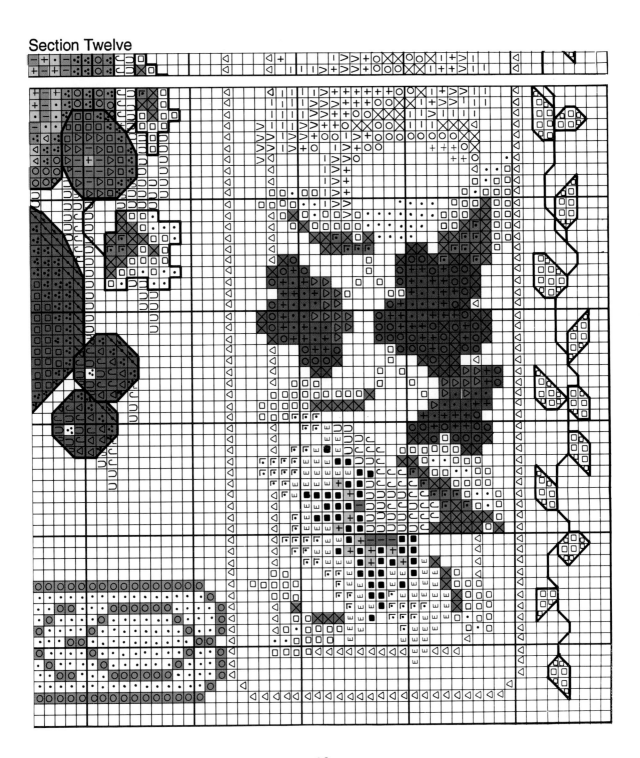

Glassworks

Stitched on pewter Jubilee 28 over two threads, the finished design size is 11" x 16⅛". The fabric was cut 17" x 23". See diagram below for graph page placement. Frame piece as desired.

FABRICS	DESIGN SIZES
Aida 11	14" x 20⅝"
Aida 14	1" x 16¼"
Aida 18	8½" x 12⅝"
Hardanger 22	7" x 10⅜"

Stitch Count: 154 x 227

Section One (page 28)	Section Two (page 29)	Section Three (page 30)	Section Four (page 31)
Section Five (page 32)	Section Six (page 33)	Section Seven (page 34)	Section Eight (page 35)
Section Nine (page 36)	Section Ten (page 37)	Section Eleven (page 38)	Section Twelve (page 39)

Top of Design

Diagram

Anchor   **DMC (used for sample)**

Step 1: Cross-stitch (2 strands)

Anchor	Symbols	DMC	Color
300	− /	745	Yellow-lt. pale
891	△ △	676	Old Gold-lt.
306	+ +	725	Topaz
307	O ◔	783	Christmas Gold
901	✕ ✕	680	Old Gold-dk.
357	□ ◹	801	Coffee Brown-dk.
323	◢ ◢	722	Orange Spice-lt.
324	◇ ◇	721	Orange Spice-med.
326	● ◔	720	Orange Spice-dk.
8	▣ ◢	353	Peach
9	+ +	352	Coral-lt.
10	O ◔	351	Coral
11	✕ ✕	350	Coral-med.
19	− −	817	Coral Red-vy. dk.
47	□ ◹	321	Christmas Red
43	⁚ ◢	815	Garnet-med.
72	◢ ◢	902	Garnet-vy. dk.
48	I	818	Baby Pink
24	∴	776	Pink-med.
69	U ◢	3687	Mauve
882	Λ	3064	Pecan-lt.

Anchor	Symbols	DMC	Color
914	− /	3772	Pecan-med.
1	+ +		White
397	• ◔	453	Shell Gray-lt.
398	△ △	452	Shell Gray-med.
399	✕ ✕	451	Shell Gray-dk.
105	⌐ ⌐	209	Lavender-dk.
185	▪ ◢	964	Seagreen-lt.
186	◇ ◇	959	Seagreen-med.
154	I I	3755	Baby Blue
978	⁙ ◢	322	Navy Blue-vy. lt.
147	O ◔	312	Navy Blue-lt.
265	I ◢	3348	Yellow Green-lt.
266	▽ ◢	3347	Yellow Green-med.
268	◢ ◢	3345	Hunter Green-dk.
214	•	368	Pistachio Green-lt.
216	□ ◹	367	Pistachio Green-dk.
246	✕ ◢	319	Pistachio Green-vy. dk.
400	⁙ ◢	317	Pewter Gray
99	▣	552	Violet-dk.
101	■	550	Violet-vy. dk.

Step 2: Blended Cross-stitch (1 strand each)

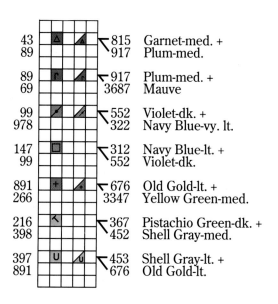

150 / 246	823 / 319	Navy Blue-dk. + Pistachio Green-vy. dk.
105 / 48	209 / 818	Lavender-dk. + Baby Pink
48 / 24	818 / 776	Baby Pink + Pink-med.
99 / 101	552 / 550	Violet-dk. + Violet-vy. dk.
306 / 300	725 / 745	Topaz + Yellow-lt. pale
8 / 9	353 / 352	Peach + Coral-lt.
300 / 8	745 / 353	Yellow-lt. pale + Peach
891 / 9	676 / 352	Old Gold-lt. + Coral-lt.
307 / 10	783 / 351	Christmas Gold + Coral
19 / 326	817 / 720	Coral Red-vy. dk. + Orange Spice-dk.
8 / 882	353 / 3064	Peach + Pecan-lt.
914 / 99	3772 / 552	Pecan-med. + Violet-dk.
147 / 43	312 / 815	Navy Blue-lt. + Garnet-med.
43 / 150	815 / 823	Garnet-med. + Navy Blue-dk.
186 / 978	959 / 322	Seagreen-med. + Navy Blue-vy. lt.
357 / 101	801 / 550	Coffee Brown-dk. + Violet-vy. dk.
216 / 266	367 / 3347	Pistachio Green-dk. + Yellow Green-med.
216 / 268	367 / 3345	Pistachio Green-dk. + Hunter Green-dk.

43 / 89	815 / 917	Garnet-med. + Plum-med.
89 / 69	917 / 3687	Plum-med. + Mauve
99 / 978	552 / 322	Violet-dk. + Navy Blue-vy. lt.
147 / 99	312 / 552	Navy Blue-lt. + Violet-dk.
891 / 266	676 / 3347	Old Gold-lt. + Yellow Green-med.
216 / 398	367 / 452	Pistachio Green-dk. + Shell Gray-med.
397 / 891	453 / 676	Shell Gray-lt. + Old Gold-lt.

Step 3: Backstitch (1 strand)

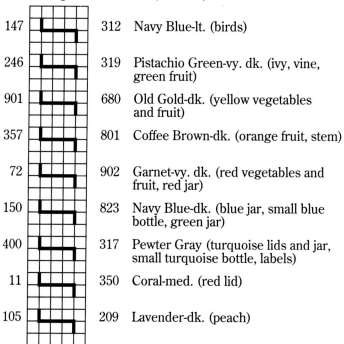

147	312	Navy Blue-lt. (birds)
246	319	Pistachio Green-vy. dk. (ivy, vine, green fruit)
901	680	Old Gold-dk. (yellow vegetables and fruit)
357	801	Coffee Brown-dk. (orange fruit, stem)
72	902	Garnet-vy. dk. (red vegetables and fruit, red jar)
150	823	Navy Blue-dk. (blue jar, small blue bottle, green jar)
400	317	Pewter Gray (turquoise lids and jar, small turquoise bottle, labels)
11	350	Coral-med. (red lid)
105	209	Lavender-dk. (peach)

Tote Bag

Stitched on Waste Canvas 16 over one thread, the finished design size is 9¼" x 1½". The fabric was cut 12" x 5". The design is the bottom border of the large framed piece and is taken from the graphs on pages 31, 35, and 39. Center waste canvas on purchased tote bag. Add ribbon or trim as shown or as desired.

FABRICS	DESIGN SIZES
Aida 11	13⅜" x 2¼"
Aida 14	10½" x 1¾"
Aida 18	8⅛" x 1⅜"
Hardanger 22	6⅝" x 1⅛"

Mirror Mat

Stitched on white Cashel Linen 28 over two threads, the finished design size is 11" x 16¼". Shown on 16" x 20" mat board, the fabric was cut 17" x 23". The design is the outside border of the large framed piece and is taken from the graphs on pages 28-39. Have mat professionally cut with the opening ½" smaller all around than design border. Cover board; frame as desired.

FABRICS	DESIGN SIZES
Aida 11	14" x 20⅝"
Aida 14	11" x 16¼"
Aida 18	8½" x 12⅝"
Hardanger 22	7" x 10⅜"

Bread Cover

Stitched on a 14-count yellow bread cover over one thread, the finished design size is 15¼" x 15¼". The design is the side border of the large framed piece and is taken from the graphs on pages 29-31. Find first stitch by matching stars on graph on page 31. Begin first stitch 1½" from woven edge of fabric. Stitch border to halfway star on page 29, reverse and repeat to finish one side of border. Rotate cloth and repeat on each remaining edge. See page 143 for supplier.

FABRICS	DESIGN SIZES
Aida 11	11¾" x 21½"
Aida 14	9¼" x 9⅞"
Aida 18	7⅛" x 7⅝"
Hardanger 22	5⅞" x 6¼"

The tiniest dewdrop
hanging from a
grass blade in the
morning is big
enough to reflect the
sunshine and the
blue of the sky.

–Unknown

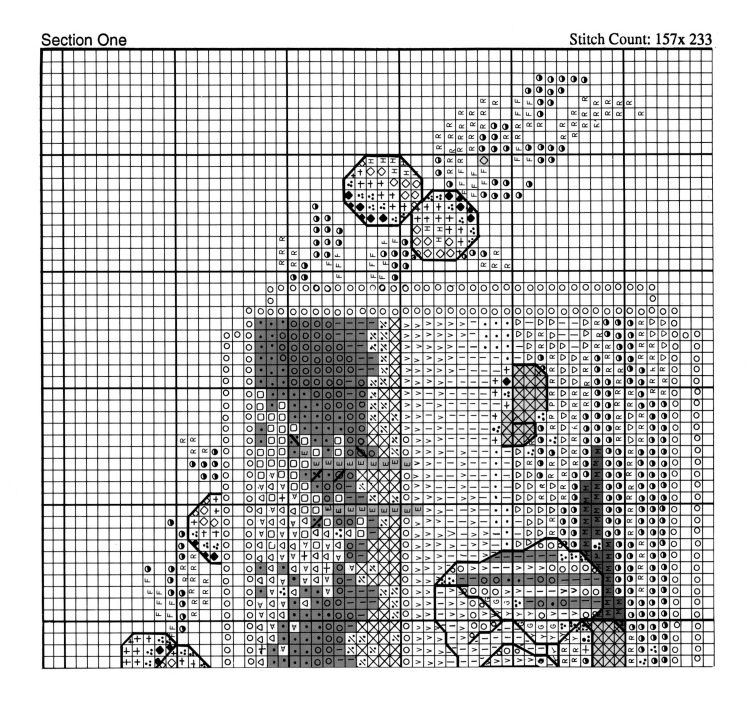

Section Two

49

Section Three

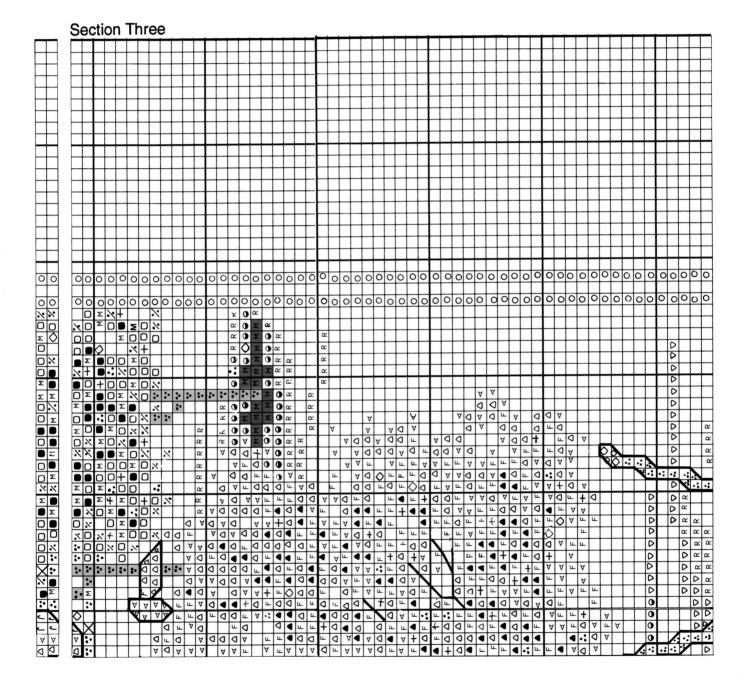

Section Four

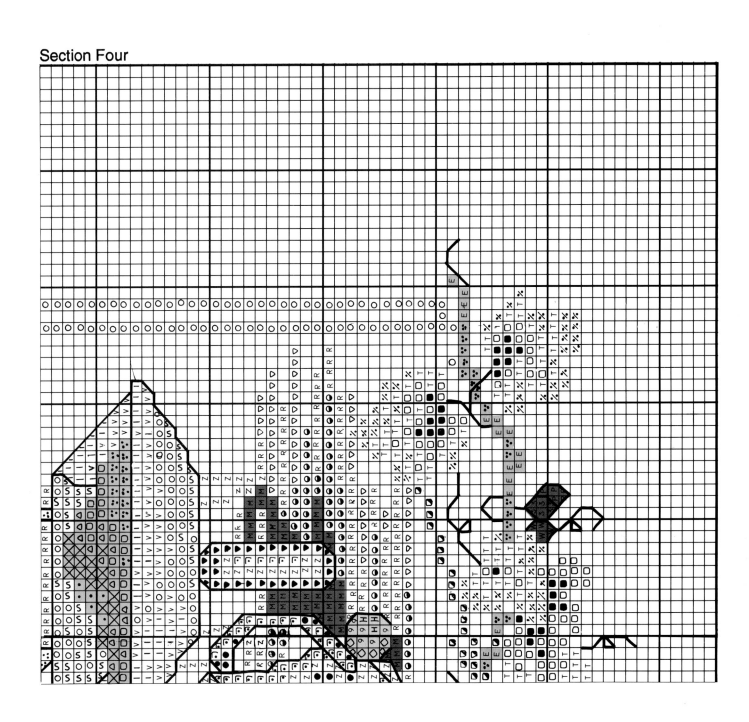

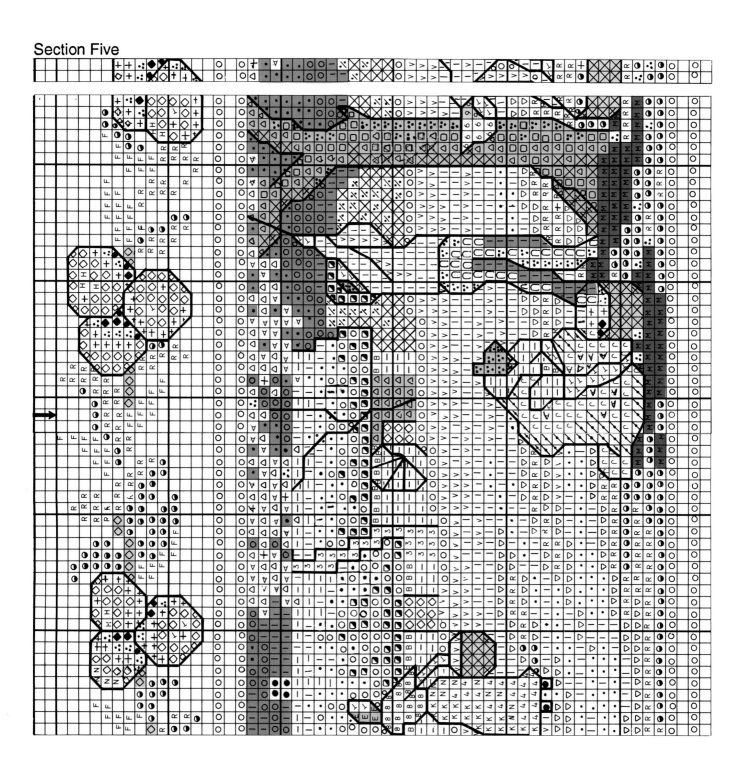

52

Section Six

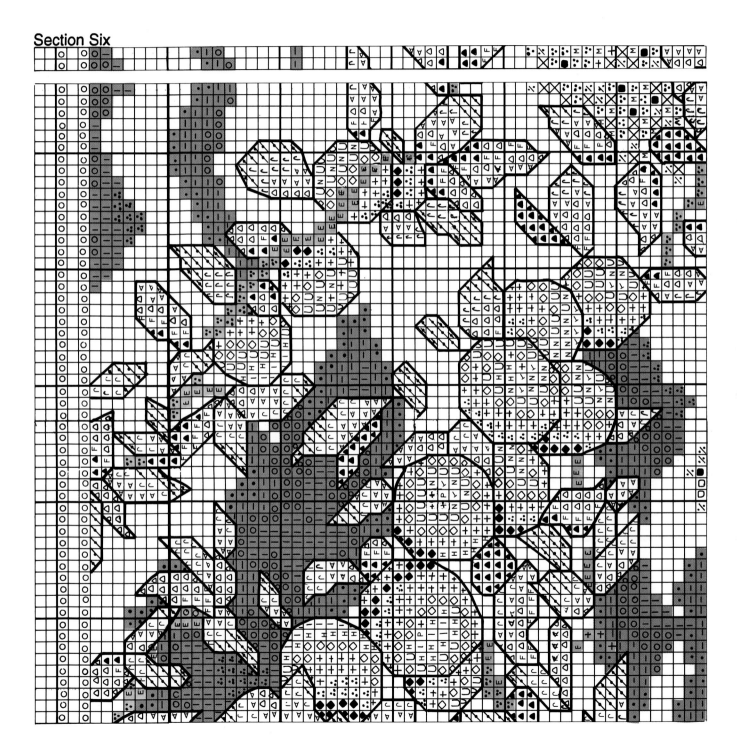

Section Seven

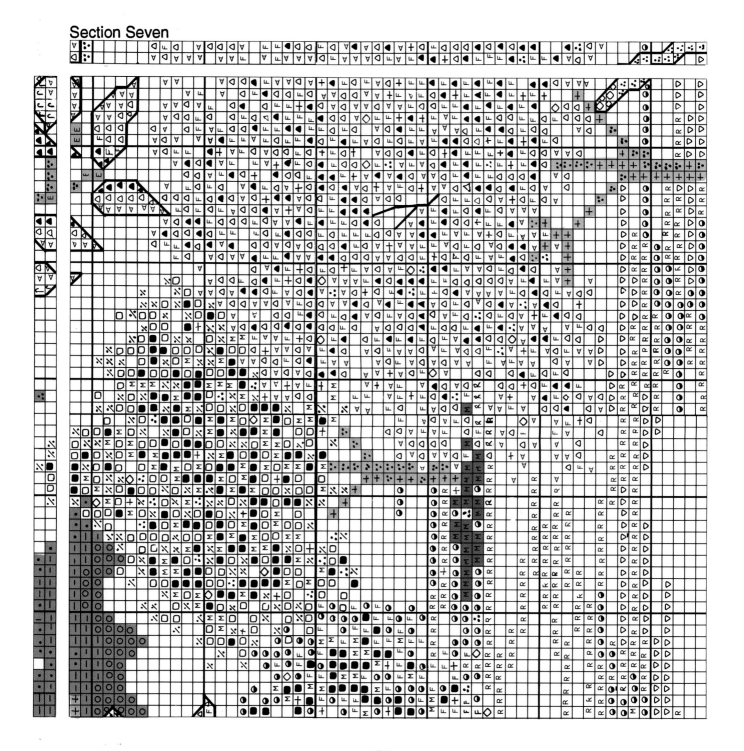

Section Eight

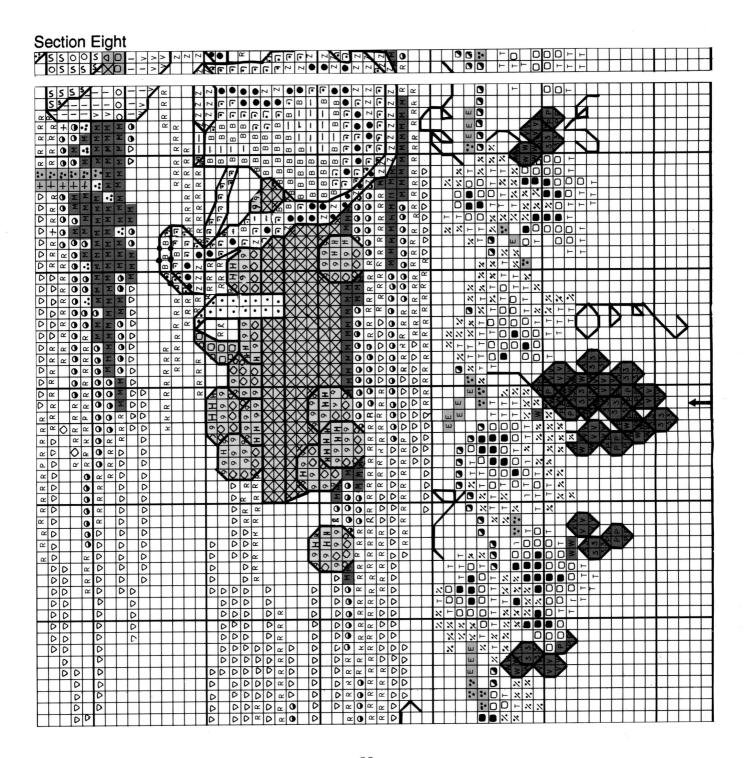

55

Section Nine

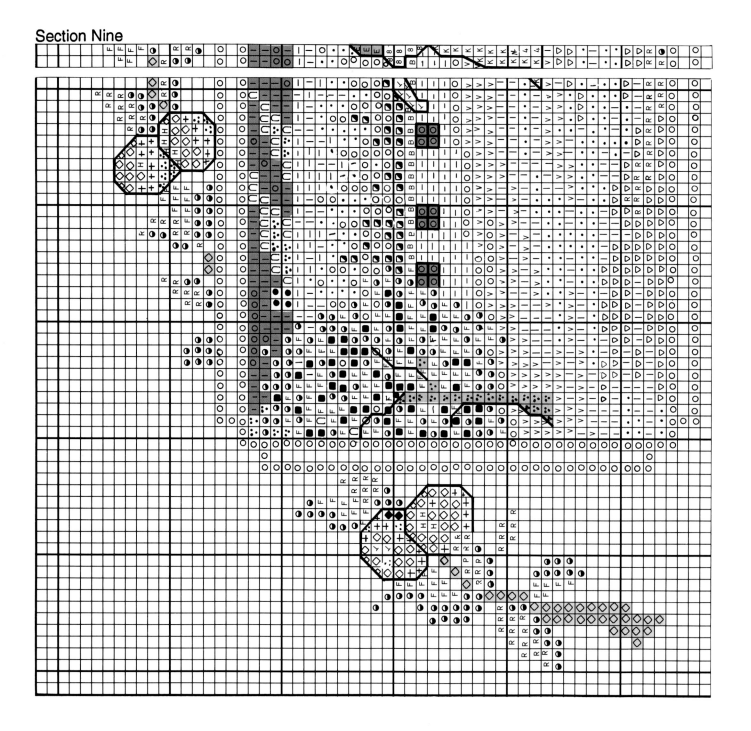

Section Ten

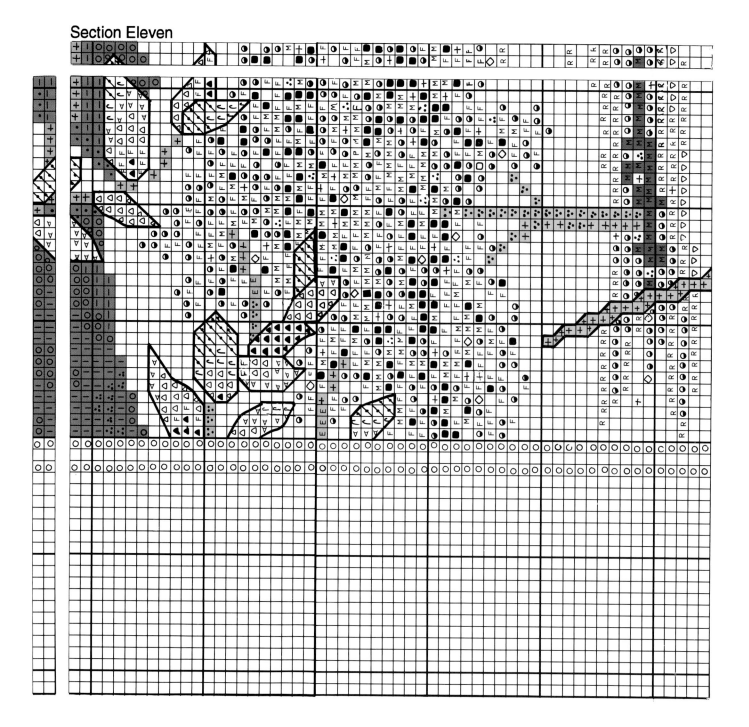

Section Twelve

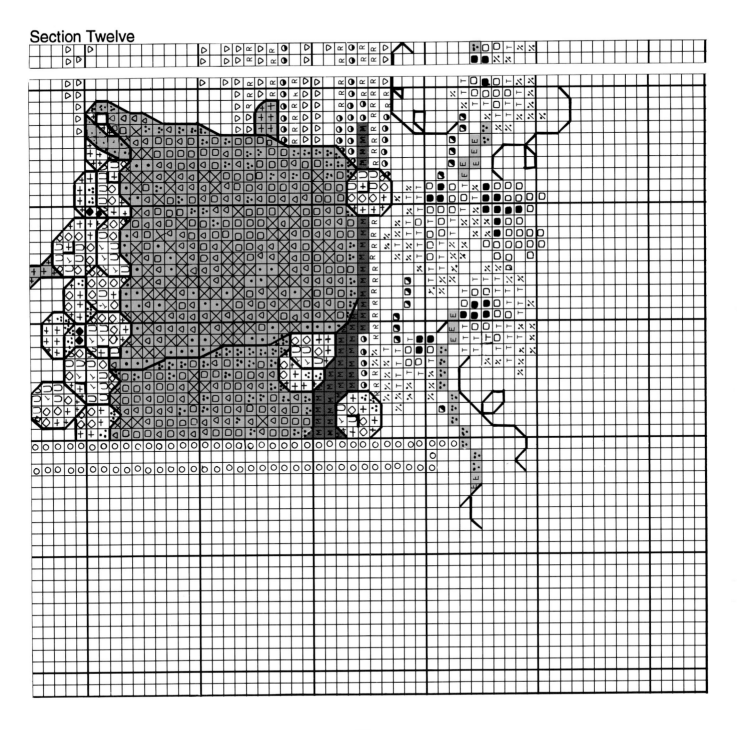

Apple Orchard

Stitched on antique white Belfast Linen 32
over two threads, the finished design size is
14½" x 9¾". The fabric was cut 16" x 21". See
diagram below for graph page placement. Frame
piece as desired.

FABRICS	DESIGN SIZES
Aida 11	14¼" x 21⅛"
Aida 14	11¼" x 16⅝"
Aida 18	8¾" x 13"
Hardanger 22	7⅛" x 10⅝"

Stitch Count: 157 x 233

Section One (page 48)	Section Two (page 49)	Section Three (page 50)	Section Four (page 51)
Section Five (page 52)	Section Six (page 53)	Section Seven (page 54)	Section Eight (page 55)
Section Nine (page 56)	Section Ten (page 57)	Section Eleven (page 58)	Section Twelve (page 59)

Top of Design

Diagram

Anchor **DMC (used for sample)**

Step 1: Cross-stitch (2 strands)

Anchor			DMC	Name
1	−	⁄		White
399	⊡	⁄	452	Shell Gray-med.
400	●	⁄	414	Steel Gray-dk.
942	·	⁄	738	Tan-vy. lt.
363	◩	⁄	436	Tan
300	I	⁄	745	Yellow-lt. pale
891	V	⁄	676	Old Gold-lt.
890	○	⁄	729	Old Gold-med.
901	∼	⁄	680	Old Gold-dk.
306	6	⁄	725	Topaz
307	9	⁄	977	Golden Brown-lt.
370	+	⁄	434	Brown-lt.
357	∴	⁄	801	Coffee Brown-dk.
105	V	⁄	209	Lavender-dk.
99	P	⁄	552	Violet-dk.
119	8	⁄	3746	Blue Violet-dk.
4146	✓	⁄	754	Peach-lt.
11	◇	⁄	350	Coral-med.
19	+	⁄	817	Coral Red-vy. dk.
22	∴	⁄	816	Garnet
44	◆	⁄	814	Garnet-dk.
9	N	⁄	760	Salmon

Anchor			DMC	Name
13	K	⁄	3328	Salmon-dk.
158	·	⁄	3756	Baby Blue-ultra vy. lt.
128	○	⁄	800	Delft-pale
130	I	⁄	809	Delft
921	∩	⁄	931	Antique Blue-med.
922	∴	⁄	930	Antique Blue-dk.
876	⁒	⁄	502	Blue Green
878	×	⁄	501	Blue Green-dk.
879	■	⁄	500	Blue Green-vy. dk.
212	□	⁄	561	Jade-vy. dk.
264	⁄	⁄	772	Pine Green-lt.
266	◁	⁄	3347	Yellow Green-med.
257	△		3346	Hunter Green
862	F		3362	Pine Green-dk.
269	▲	⁄	935	Avocado Green-dk.
843	R	⁄	3364	Pine Green
861	◓	⁄	3363	Pine Green-med.
379	△	⁄	840	Beige Brown-med.
11	U	⁄	351	Coral
338	◇	⁄	3776	Mahogany-lt.
978	∴	⁄	322	Navy Blue-vy. lt.

61

Step 2: Blended Cross-stitch (1 strand each)

357 / 379	801 / 840	Coffee Brown-dk. + Beige Brown-med.
379 / 942	840 / 738	Beige Brown-med. + Tan-vy. lt.
370 / 357	434 / 801	Brown-lt. + Coffee Brown-dk.
9 / 13	760 / 3328	Salmon + Salmon-dk.
22 / 922	816 / 930	Garnet + Antique Blue-dk.
901 / 105	680 / 209	Old Gold-dk. + Lavender-dk.
1 / 399	452	White + Shell Gray-med.
400 / 363	414 / 436	Steel Gray-dk. + Tan
306 / 9	725 / 760	Topaz + Salmon
264 / 266	772 / 3347	Pine Green-lt. + Yellow Green-med.
44 / 150	814 / 823	Garnet-dk. + Navy Blue-dk.
400 / 922	414 / 930	Steel Gray-dk. + Antique Blue-dk.
862 / 99	3362 / 552	Pine Green-dk. + Violet-dk.
300 / 843	745 / 3364	Yellow-lt. pale + Pine Green
876 / 212	502 / 561	Blue Green + Jade-vy. dk.
300 / 1	745	Yellow-lt. pale + White
307 / 300	977 / 745	Golden Brown-lt. + Yellow-lt. pale
150 / 879	823 / 500	Navy Blue-dk. + Blue Green-vy. dk.
257 / 922	3346 / 930	Hunter Green + Antique Blue-dk.
9 / 105	760 / 209	Salmon + Lavender-dk.

101 / 22	550 / 816	Violet-vy. dk. + Garnet
128 / 158	800 / 3756	Delft-pale + Baby Blue-ultra vy. lt.
370 / 942	434 / 738	Brown-lt. + Tan-vy. lt.

Step 3: Backstitch (1 strand)

44	814	Garnet-dk. (apples, wheelbarrow handles)
357	801	Coffee Brown-dk. (oranges, rake, basket, tree, tree limbs, hair, hat)
862	3362	Pine Green-dk. (leaves)
150	823	Navy Blue-dk. (wheelbarrow tire, purple blouse, blue pants, watering can)
400	414	Steel Gray-dk. (wheelbarrow body, windows, doors, shoe, green dress, white blouse, headscarf)
22	816	Garnet (grapes)
212	561	Jade-vy. dk. (grape vines)
338	3776	Mahogany-lt. (arms, faces)
370	434	Brown-lt. (roof, wheel against house)
13	3328	Salmon-dk. (light red skirt)
399	452	Shell Gray-med. (pale yellow shirt, pale yellow blouse)

Step 4: Straight-stitch (2 strands)

357	801	Coffee Brown-dk. (stick in man's hand)
370	434	Brown-lt. (inside of wheel against house)

Step 5: French Knot (1 strand)

150	823	Navy Blue-dk. (watering can)

Box Top

Stitched on mocha Belfast Linen 32 over two threads, the finished design size is 6⅛" x 2¼". The fabric was cut 11" x 7". The design is the top section of the large framed piece and is taken from the graphs on pages 48, 52, and 56. Paint box if desired, then follow manufacturer's instructions for inserting stitching. See page 143 for supplier.

FABRICS	DESIGN SIZES
Aida 11	8⅞" x 3⅜"
Aida 14	7" x 2⅝"
Aida 18	5⅛" x 2"
Hardanger 22	4½" x 1⅝"

Towel Border

Stitched on a 14-count towel over one thread, the finished design size is 9⅜" x 2¼". The design is the grapevine section of the large framed piece and is taken from the graphs on pages 51, 55, and 59. Center design on purchased towel. See page 143 for supplier.

FABRICS	DESIGN SIZES
Aida 11	12" x 2⅞"
Aida 14	9⅜" x 2¼"
Aida 18	7⅜" x 1¾"
Hardanger 22	6" x 1⅜"

Bottle Band

Stitched on cream Belfast Linen 32 over two threads, the finished design size is 5" x 3½". The fabric was cut 16" x 8". The design is the apple branch from the large framed piece and is taken from the graphs on pages 49, 53, and 57. Measure 2⅛" down from top edge and 6" in from left edge of fabric to place first stitch. Find first and last stitches by connecting stars on graphs on pages 57 and 49. Hem and edge with narrow piping as desired.

FABRICS	DESIGN SIZES
Aida 11	7⅛" x 5⅛"
Aida 14	5⅝" x 4⅛"
Aida 18	4⅜" x 3⅛"
Hardanger 22	3⅝" x 2⅝"

For the winter is past,
the rain is over and
gone. The flowers are
springing up and the
time of the singing
birds has come.
Yes, Spring is here.

–Song of Solomon 2:11-12

Wings

Be like the bird
That, pausing in her flight
Awhile on boughs too slight,
Feels them give way
Beneath her and yet sings,
Knowing that she hath wi

Victor Hug

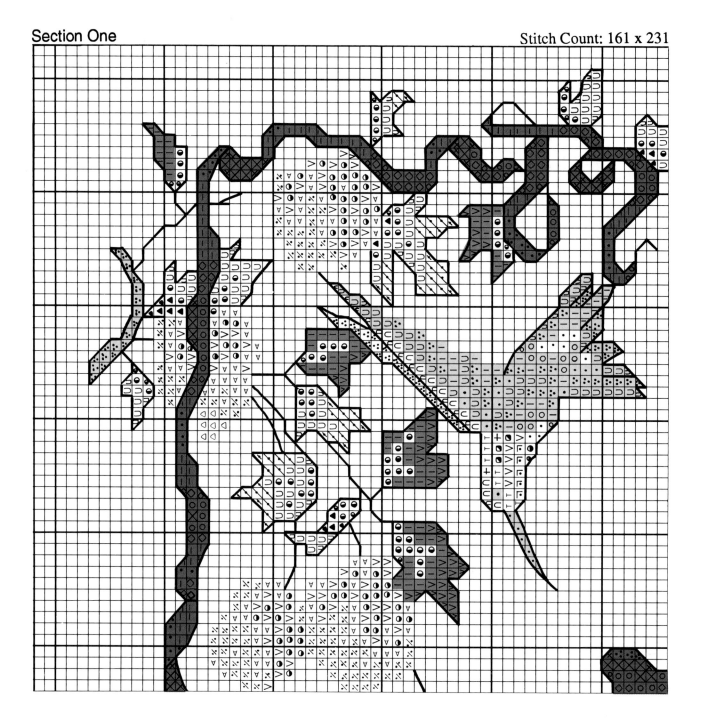

Section Two

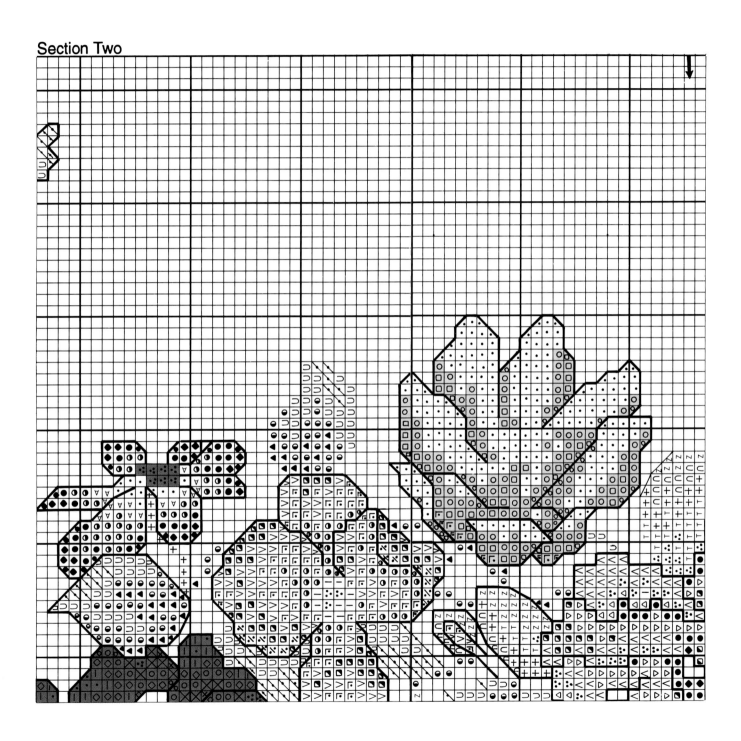

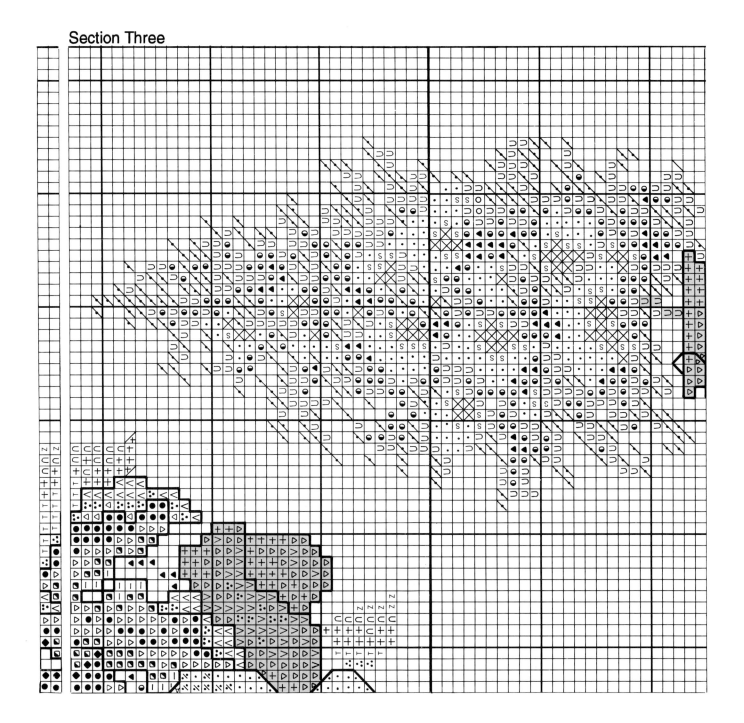

Section Four

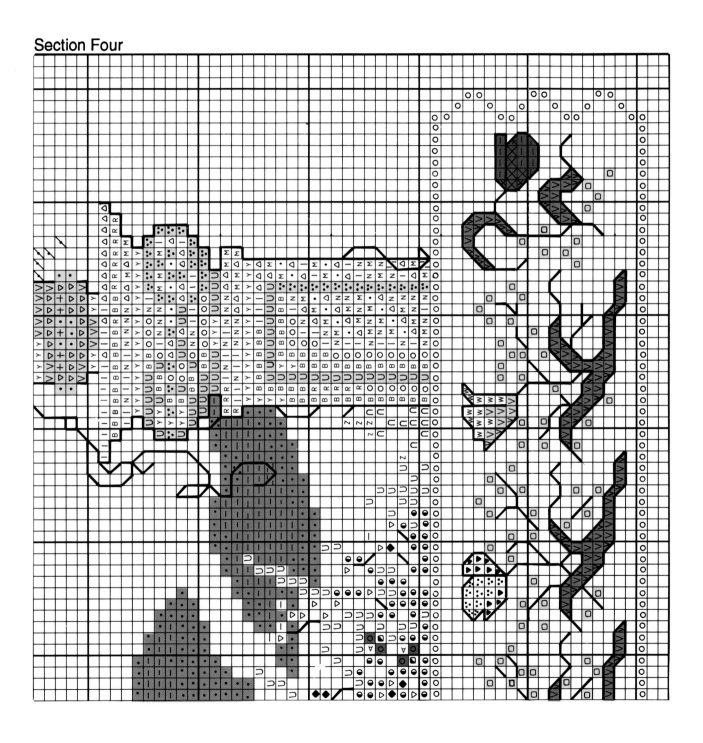

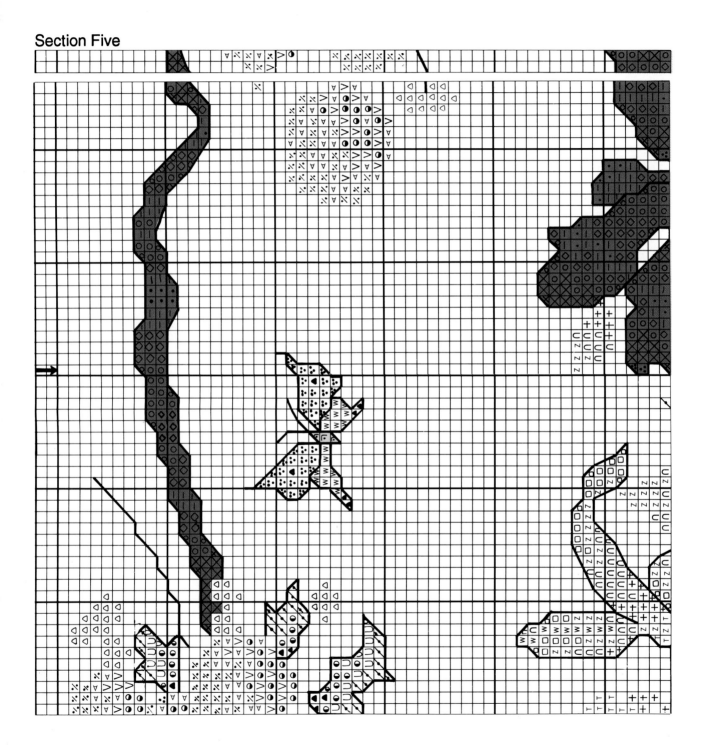

72

Section Six

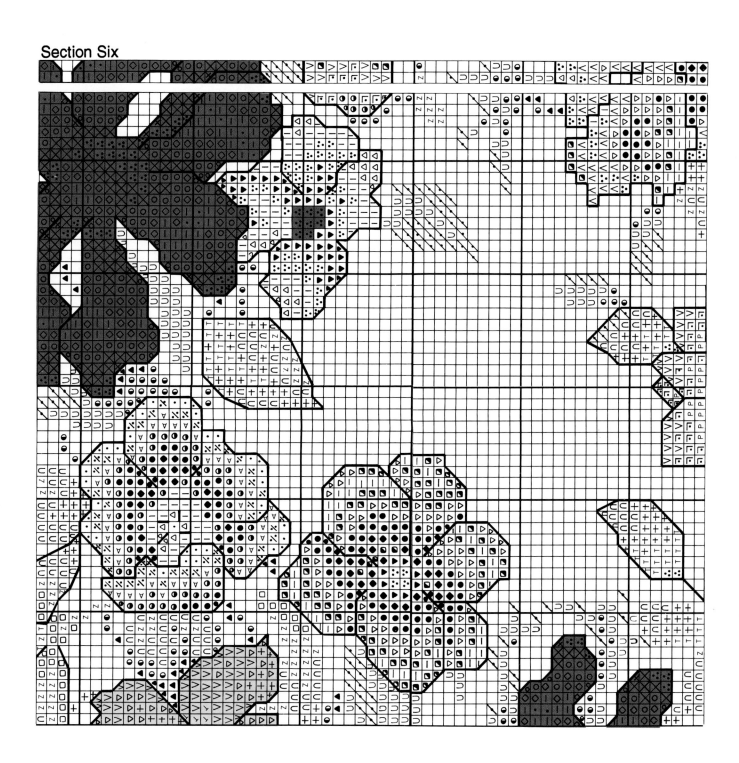

Section Seven

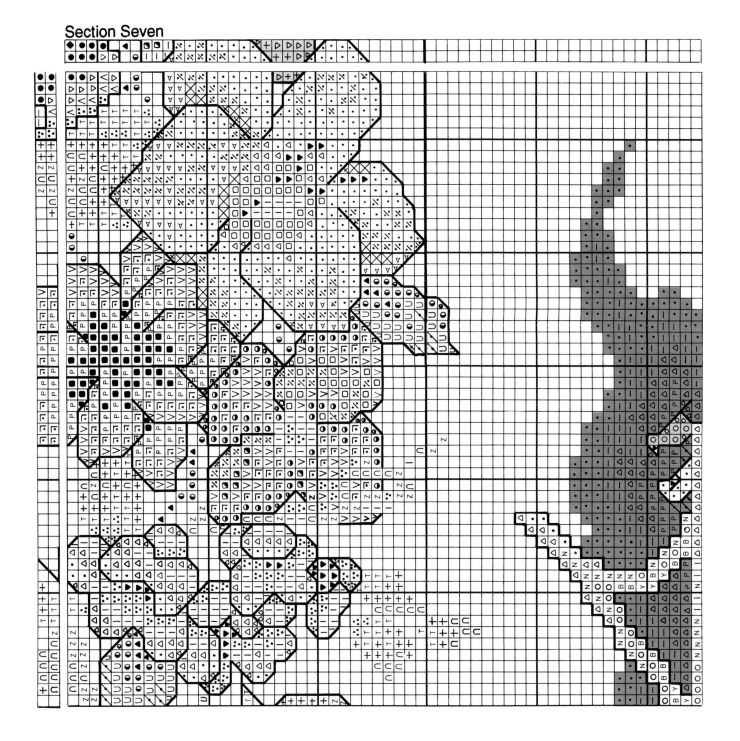

Section Eight

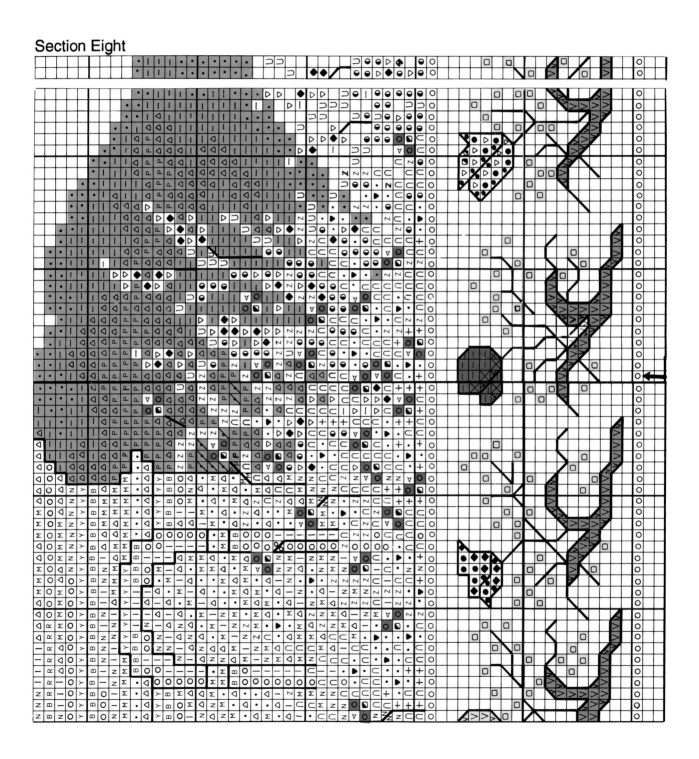

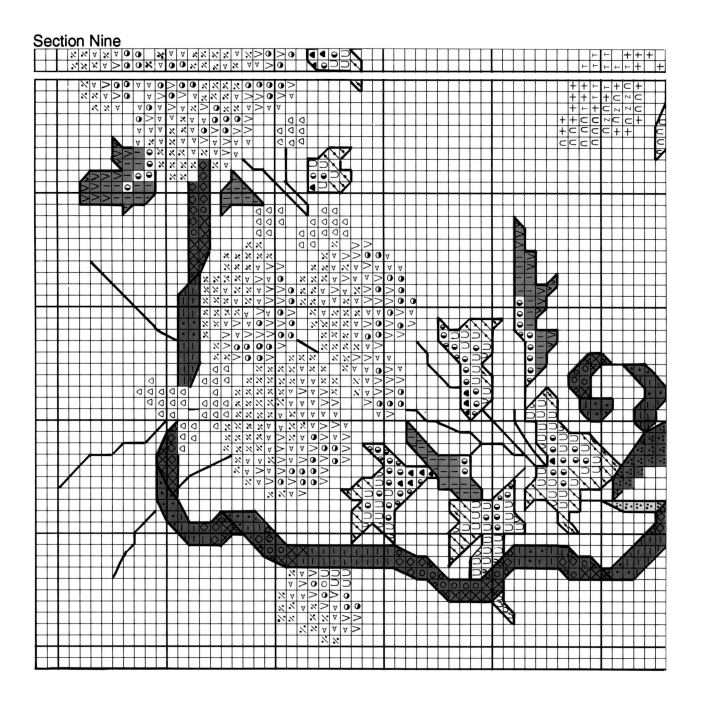

Section Ten

Section Eleven

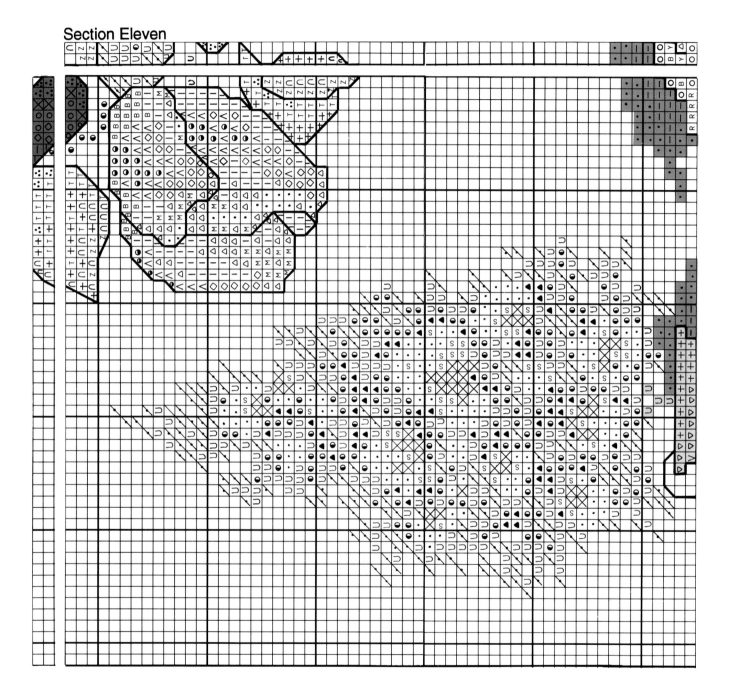

Section Twelve

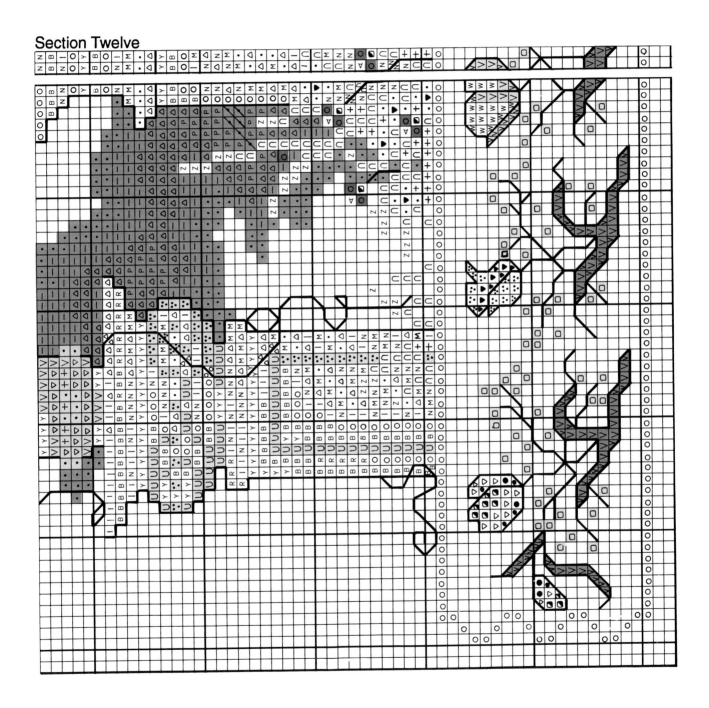

Nature's Song

Stitched on cameo peach Jobelan 28 over two threads, the finished design size is 11⅜" x 16⅜". The fabric was cut 18" x 23". See diagram below for graph page placement. Frame piece as desired.

FABRICS | DESIGN SIZES
Aida 11 | 14½" x 21"
Aida 14 | 11⅜" x 16½"
Aida 18 | 8⅞" x 12⅞"
Hardanger 22 | 7¼" x 10½"

Stitch Count: 161 x 231

Section One (page 68)	Section Two (page 69)	Section Three (page 70)	Section Four (page 71)
Section Five (page 72)	Section Six (page 73)	Section Seven (page 74)	Section Eight (page 75)
Section Nine (page 76)	Section Ten (page 77)	Section Eleven (page 78)	Section Twelve (page 79)

Top of Design

Diagram

Anchor   **DMC (used for sample)**

Step 1: Cross-stitch (2 strands)

Anchor			DMC	Color
1	·	⁄		White
300	△	△⁄	745	Yellow-lt. pale
891	I	⁄I	676	Old Gold-lt.
306	∴	⁄∴	725	Topaz
307	▼		783	Christmas Gold
307	W	W⁄	977	Golden Brown-lt.
338	V		3776	Mahogany-lt.
885	M	M⁄	739	Tan-ultra vy. lt.
942	N	N⁄	738	Tan-vy. lt.
363	R	R⁄	436	Tan
379	I	⁄	840	Beige Brown-med.
381	·	⁄·	838	Beige Brown-vy. dk.
397	○	⁄○	453	Shell Gray-lt.
399	◙	⁄◙	451	Shell Gray-dk.
158	·		3756	Baby Blue-ultra vy. lt.
159	△		3325	Baby Blue-lt.
154	◢		3755	Baby Blue
121	I	⁄I	793	Cornflower Blue-med.
940	%	⁄%	792	Cornflower Blue-dk.
265	Z	Z⁄	3348	Yellow Green-lt.
266	∩	∩⁄	3347	Yellow Green-med.
257	+	+⁄	3346	Hunter Green
862	∴	⁄∴	935	Avocado Green-dk.
215	⁄	⁄⁄	320	Pistachio Green-med.
216	U	U⁄	367	Pistachio Green-dk.
246	◖	⁄◖	319	Pistachio Green-vy. dk.
876	V	V⁄	502	Blue Green

Anchor			DMC	Color
878	I	⁄I	501	Blue Green-dk.
66	■	⁄■	3608	Plum-vy. lt.
69	─	⁄─	3607	Plum-lt.
89	○	⁄○	917	Plum-med.
49	%·	⁄%·	963	Wild Rose-vy. lt.
76	V	V⁄	962	Wild Rose-med.
8	◄	⁄◄	760	Salmon
9	◗	⁄◗	3328	Salmon-dk.
10	─	⁄	352	Coral-lt.
11	◢	⁄◢	351	Coral
13	▽	⁄▽	350	Coral-med.
19	●	⁄●	817	Coral Red-vy. dk.
22	◆	⁄◆	816	Garnet
44	◢	⁄◢	814	Garnet-dk.

Step 2: Blended Cross-stitch (1 strand each)

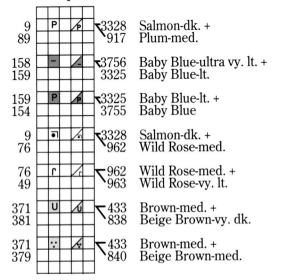

Anchor			DMC	Color
9 / 89	P	P⁄	3328 / 917	Salmon-dk. + Plum-med.
158 / 159	─	⁄─	3756 / 3325	Baby Blue-ultra vy. lt. + Baby Blue-lt.
159 / 154	P	P⁄	3325 / 3755	Baby Blue-lt. + Baby Blue
9 / 76	◙	⁄◙	3328 / 962	Salmon-dk. + Wild Rose-med.
76 / 49	⌐	⁄⌐	962 / 963	Wild Rose-med. + Wild Rose-vy. lt.
371 / 381	U	U⁄	433 / 838	Brown-med. + Beige Brown-vy. dk.
371 / 379	∴	⁄∴	433 / 840	Brown-med. + Beige Brown-med.

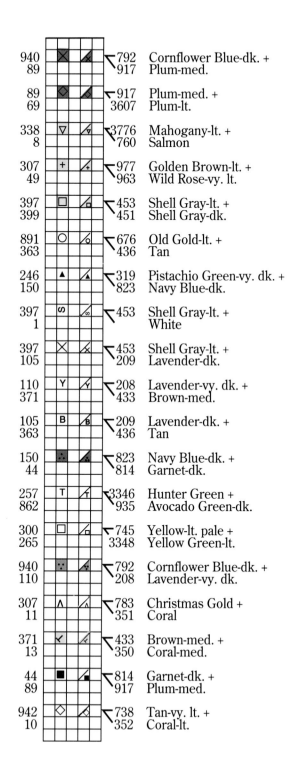

940 / 89	792 / 917	Cornflower Blue-dk. + Plum-med.
89 / 69	917 / 3607	Plum-med. + Plum-lt.
338 / 8	3776 / 760	Mahogany-lt. + Salmon
307 / 49	977 / 963	Golden Brown-lt. + Wild Rose-vy. lt.
397 / 399	453 / 451	Shell Gray-lt. + Shell Gray-dk.
891 / 363	676 / 436	Old Gold-lt. + Tan
246 / 150	319 / 823	Pistachio Green-vy. dk. + Navy Blue-dk.
397 / 1	453 / White	Shell Gray-lt. + White
397 / 105	453 / 209	Shell Gray-lt. + Lavender-dk.
110 / 371	208 / 433	Lavender-vy. dk. + Brown-med.
105 / 363	209 / 436	Lavender-dk. + Tan
150 / 44	823 / 814	Navy Blue-dk. + Garnet-dk.
257 / 862	3346 / 935	Hunter Green + Avocado Green-dk.
300 / 265	745 / 3348	Yellow-lt. pale + Yellow Green-lt.
940 / 110	792 / 208	Cornflower Blue-dk. + Lavender-vy. dk.
307 / 11	783 / 351	Christmas Gold + Coral
371 / 13	433 / 350	Brown-med. + Coral-med.
44 / 89	814 / 917	Garnet-dk. + Plum-med.
942 / 10	738 / 352	Tan-vy. lt. + Coral-lt.

Step 3: Backstitch (1 strand)

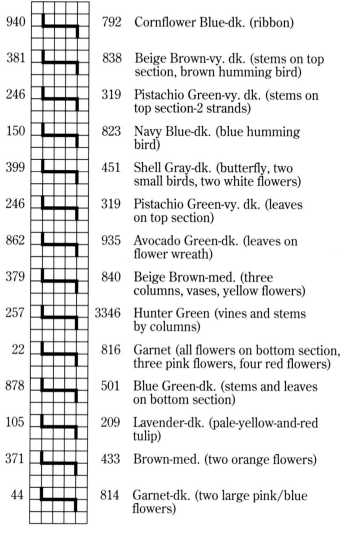

940	792	Cornflower Blue-dk. (ribbon)
381	838	Beige Brown-vy. dk. (stems on top section, brown humming bird)
246	319	Pistachio Green-vy. dk. (stems on top section-2 strands)
150	823	Navy Blue-dk. (blue humming bird)
399	451	Shell Gray-dk. (butterfly, two small birds, two white flowers)
246	319	Pistachio Green-vy. dk. (leaves on top section)
862	935	Avocado Green-dk. (leaves on flower wreath)
379	840	Beige Brown-med. (three columns, vases, yellow flowers)
257	3346	Hunter Green (vines and stems by columns)
22	816	Garnet (all flowers on bottom section, three pink flowers, four red flowers)
878	501	Blue Green-dk. (stems and leaves on bottom section)
105	209	Lavender-dk. (pale-yellow-and-red tulip)
371	433	Brown-med. (two orange flowers)
44	814	Garnet-dk. (two large pink/blue flowers)

83

Hatband

Stitched on white Murano 30 over two threads, the finished design size is 10¼" x 1". The fabric was cut 23" x 8". The design is the bottom tulip border of the large framed piece and is taken from the graphs on pages 71, 75, and 79. Center design; hem and edge with ribbon as shown or as desired.

FABRICS	DESIGN SIZES
Aida 11	13⅞" x 1⅜"
Aida 14	10⅞" x 1⅛"
Aida 18	8½" x ⅞"
Hardanger 22	7" x ⅝"

Bed Sheets

Stitched on Waste Canvas 14 over one thread, the finished design size is 6¾" x 2⅛". The fabric was cut 9" x 9". The design is the lower floral motif of the large framed piece and is taken from the graphs on pages 71, 75, and 79. Repeat motif spaced 3" apart across the top hem of the sheet with the lower edge toward the fold.

FABRICS	DESIGN SIZES
Aida 11	8½" x 2⅝"
Aida 14	6¾" x 2⅛"
Aida 18	5¼" x 1⅝"
Hardanger 22	4¼" x 1⅜"

Blouse

Stitched on Waste Canvas 14 over one thread, the finished design size is 2" x 2⅛" for hummingbird. For the tulip, finished design sizes are each approximately 1⅝" x 1". For each motif, cut and baste an appropriately sized piece of waste canvas on the blouse. The hummingbird design is on the upper right corner of the large framed piece and is taken from the graph on page 68; refer to the hatband directions at left to locate the tulips.

Hummingbird

FABRICS	DESIGN SIZES
Aida 11	2½" x 2¾"
Aida 14	2" x 2⅛"
Aida 18	1½" x 1⅝"
Hardanger 22	1¼" x 1⅜"

When in these fresh
mornings I go into
my garden before
anyone is awake, I
go for the time being
into perfect
happiness.

—*Celia Thaxter*

Stitch Count: 160 x 230

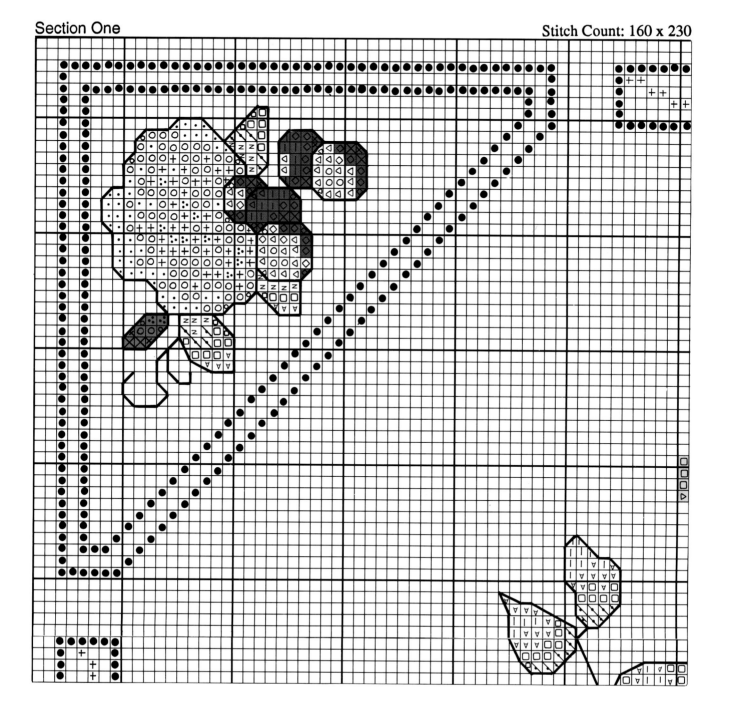

Section Two

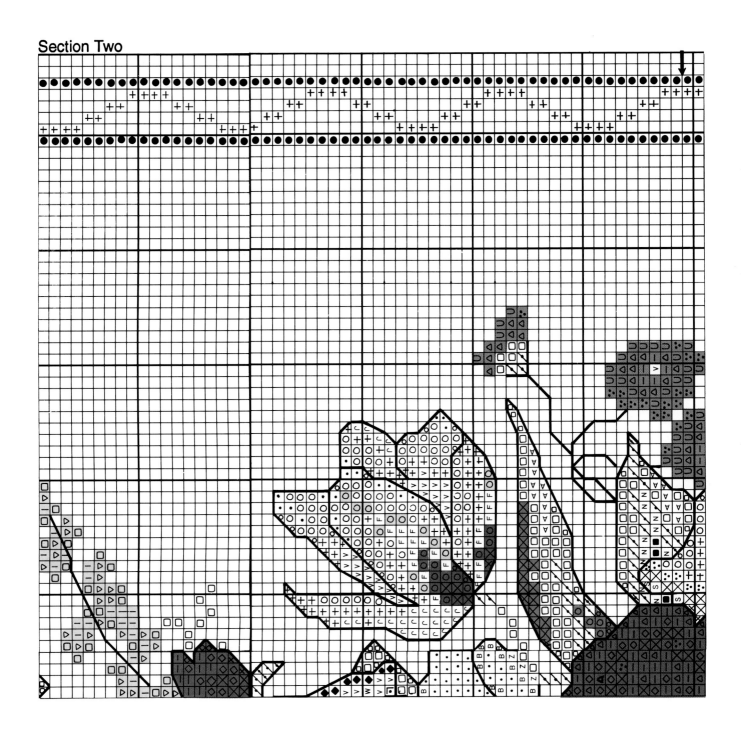

Section Three

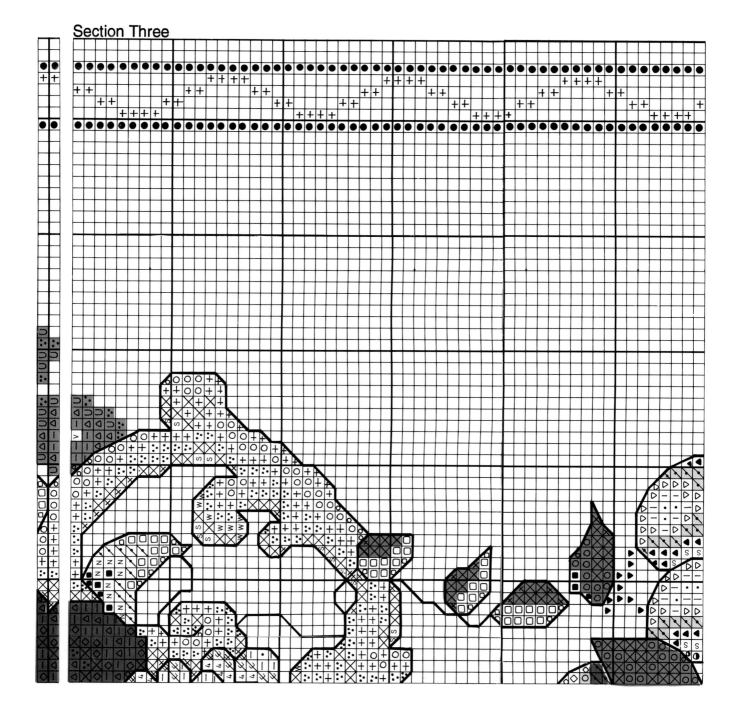

90

Section Four

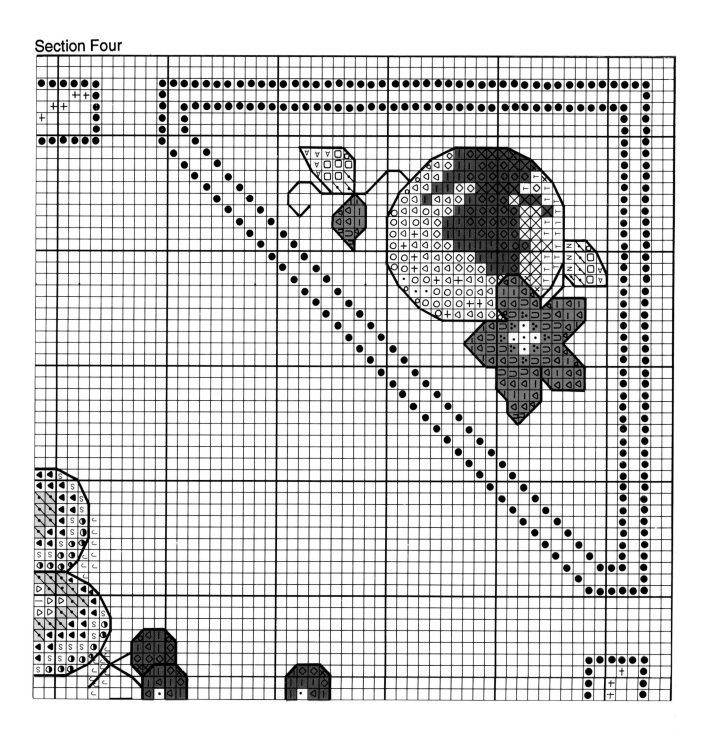

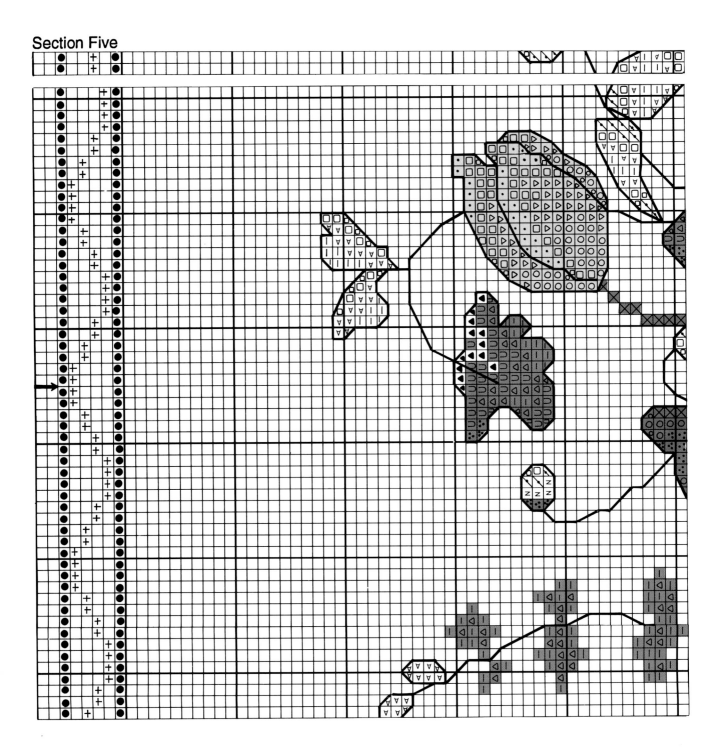

Section Six

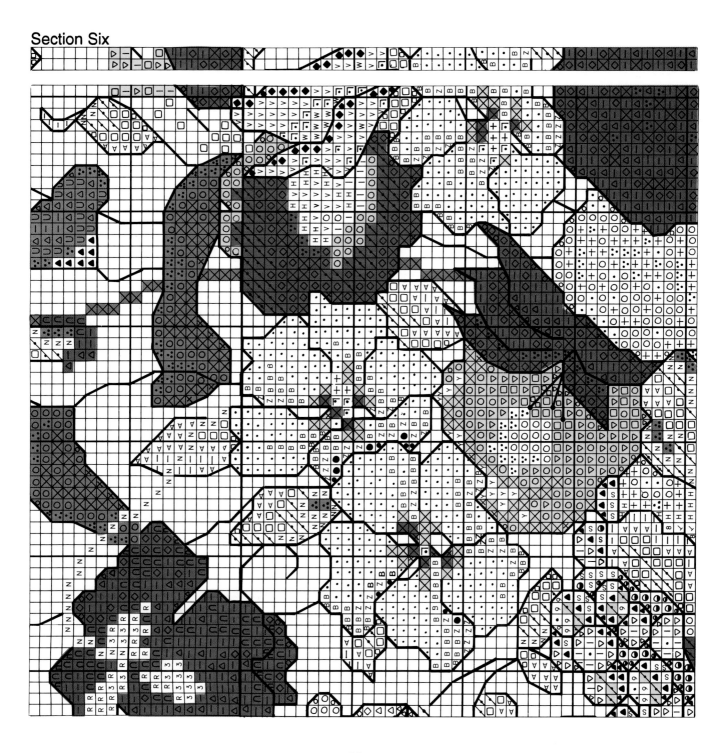

93

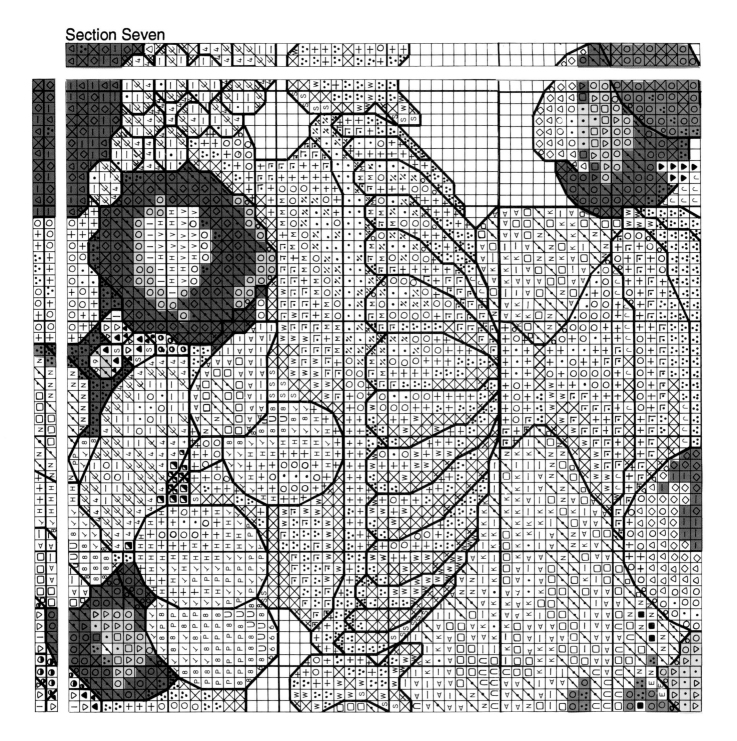

94

Section Eight

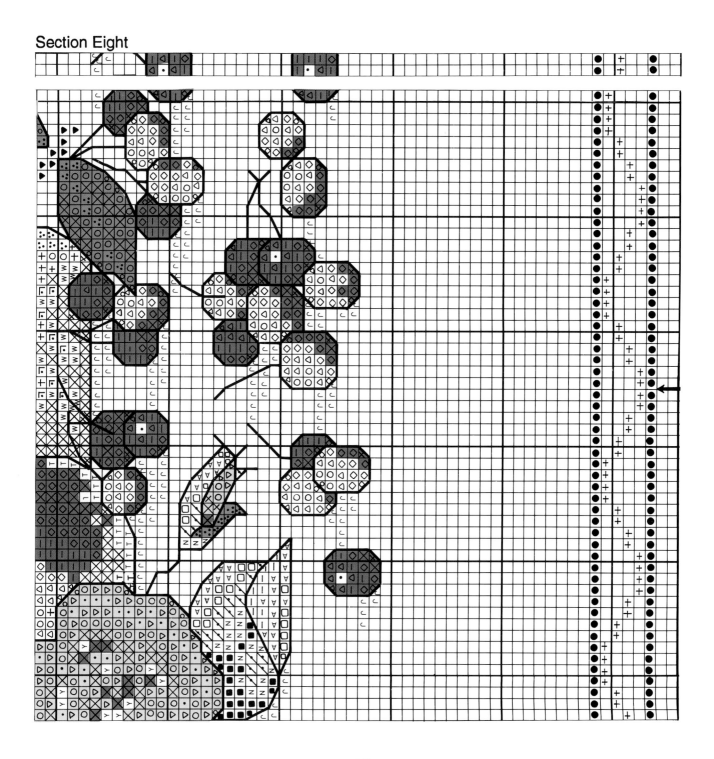

95

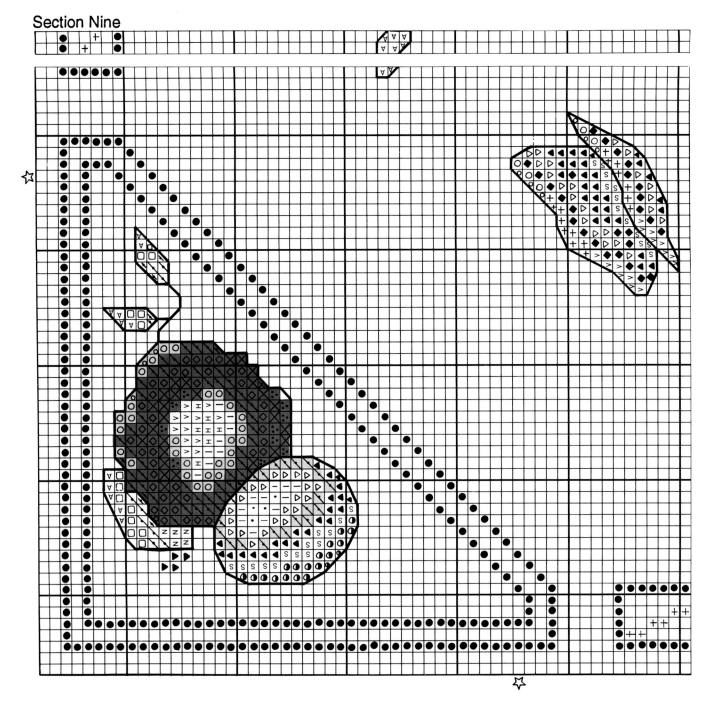

96

Section Ten

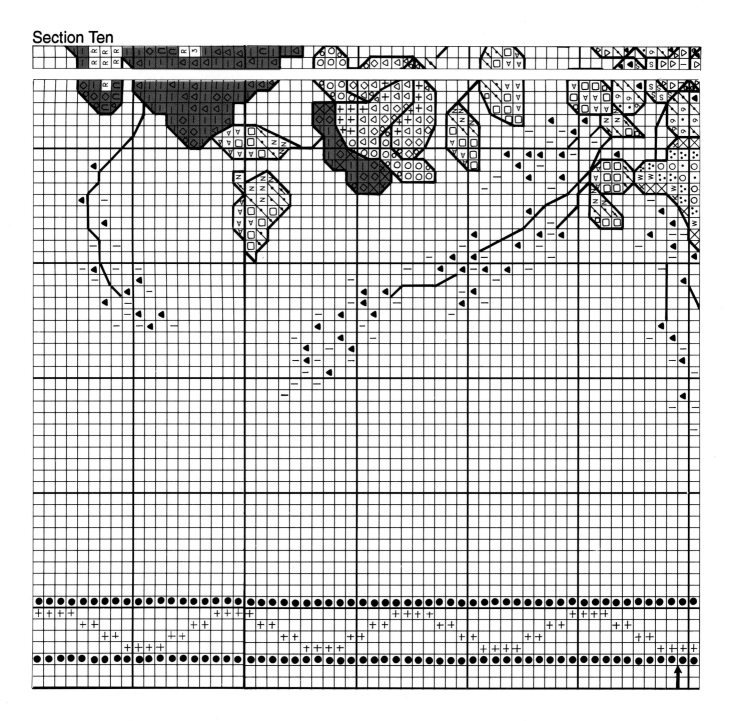

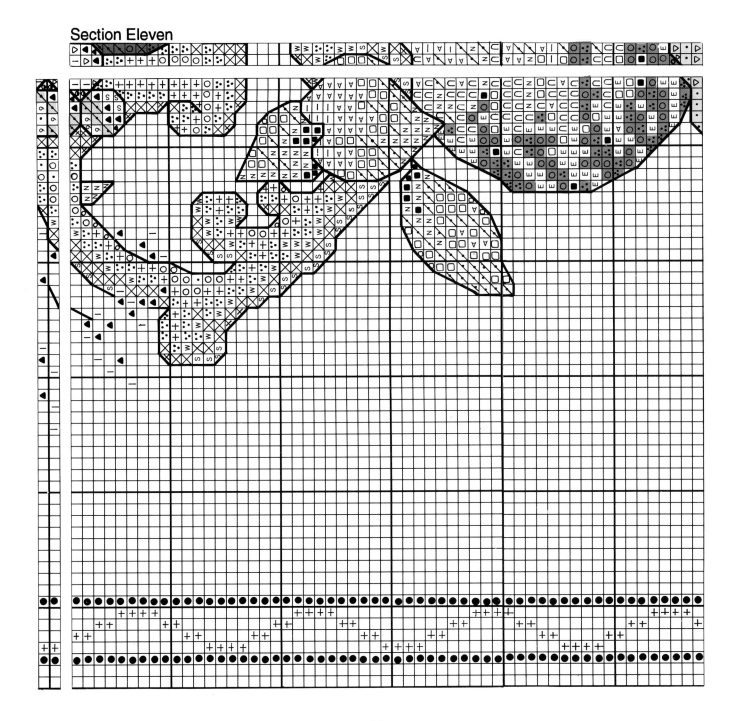

Section Twelve

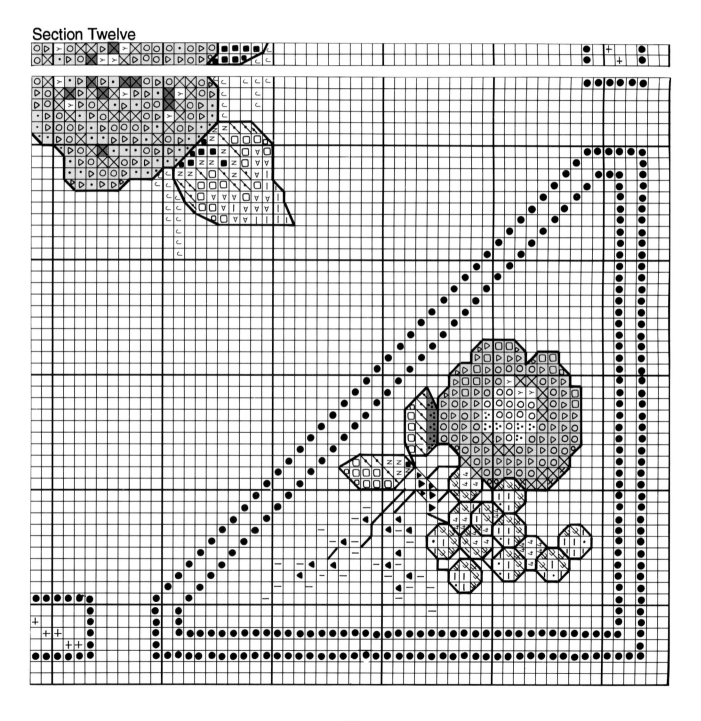

Garden Bouquet

Stitched on vintage Linen 28 over two threads, the finished design size is 11⅜" x 16⅜". The fabric was cut 18" x 23". See diagram below for graph page placement. Frame piece as desired.

FABRICS	DESIGN SIZES
Aida 11	14½" x 20⅞"
Aida 14	11⅜" x 16⅜"
Aida 18	8⅞" x 12¾"
Hardanger 22	7¼" x 10½"

Stitch Count: 160 x 230

Section One (page 88)	Section Two (page 89)	Section Three (page 90)	Section Four (page 91)
Section Five (page 92)	Section Six (page 93)	Section Seven (page 94)	Section Eight (page 95)
Section Nine (page 96)	Section Ten (page 97)	Section Eleven (page 98)	Section Twelve (page 99)

Top of Design

Diagram

100

Anchor   DMC (used for sample)

Step 1: Cross-stitch (2 strands)

Anchor			DMC	Color
1	·	⁄·		White
397	B	⁄B	3072	Beaver Gray-vy. lt.
8581	●	⁄●	647	Beaver Gray-med.
300	○	⁄○	745	Yellow-lt. pale
891	+	⁄+	676	Old Gold-lt.
890	◙	⁄◙	729	Old Gold-med.
901	W	⁄W	680	Old Gold-dk.
370	∴	⁄∴	434	Brown-lt.
357	▼	⁄▼	801	Coffee Brown-dk.
306	V	⁄V	725	Topaz
307	H	⁄H	977	Golden Brown-lt.
326	6	⁄6	720	Orange Spice-dk.
120	–	⁄	794	Cornflower Blue-lt.
121	△	⁄△	793	Cornflower Blue-med.
940	∴	⁄∴	792	Cornflower Blue-dk.
894	I	⁄I	223	Shell Pink-med.
8	·	⁄·	761	Salmon-lt.
9	○	⁄○	3712	Salmon-med.
27	▽	⁄▽	899	Rose-med.
42	✕	⁄✕	309	Rose-deep
10	△	⁄△	351	Coral
11	▤	⁄	350	Coral-med.
13	◇	⁄	349	Coral-dk.
19	◎	⁄◎	347	Salmon-vy. dk.
22	✕	⁄✕	816	Garnet
44	∴	⁄∴	814	Garnet-dk.
104	I	⁄I	210	Lavender-med.
105	▽	⁄▽	209	Lavender-dk.
99	▲	⁄▲	552	Violet-dk.

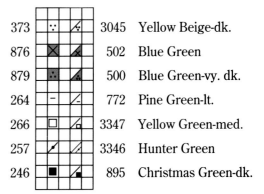

Anchor			DMC	Color
373	∴∴	⁄	3045	Yellow Beige-dk.
876	✕	⁄	502	Blue Green
879	∴	⁄	500	Blue Green-vy. dk.
264	–	⁄–	772	Pine Green-lt.
266	□	⁄□	3347	Yellow Green-med.
257	⁄	⁄	3346	Hunter Green
246	■	⁄■	895	Christmas Green-dk.

Step 2: Blended Cross-stitch (1 strand each)

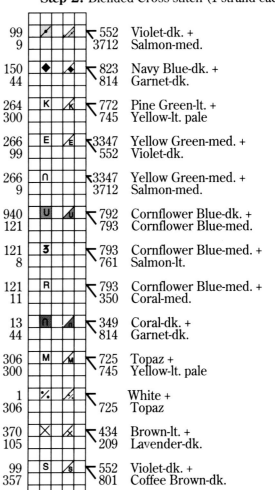

Anchor			DMC	Color
99 / 9	⁄	⁄	552 / 3712	Violet-dk. + Salmon-med.
150 / 44	◆	⁄◆	823 / 814	Navy Blue-dk. + Garnet-dk.
264 / 300	K	⁄K	772 / 745	Pine Green-lt. + Yellow-lt. pale
266 / 99	E	⁄E	3347 / 552	Yellow Green-med. + Violet-dk.
266 / 9	∩		3347 / 3712	Yellow Green-med. + Salmon-med.
940 / 121	U	⁄U	792 / 793	Cornflower Blue-dk. + Cornflower Blue-med.
121 / 8	3		793 / 761	Cornflower Blue-med. + Salmon-lt.
121 / 11	R		793 / 350	Cornflower Blue-med. + Coral-med.
13 / 44	∩	⁄	349 / 814	Coral-dk. + Garnet-dk.
306 / 300	M	⁄M	725 / 745	Topaz + Yellow-lt. pale
1 / 306	∴	⁄	/ 725	White + Topaz
370 / 105	✕	⁄✕	434 / 209	Brown-lt. + Lavender-dk.
99 / 357	S	⁄S	552 / 801	Violet-dk. + Coffee Brown-dk.

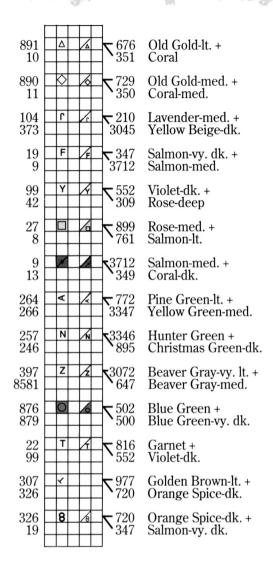

891 / 10	676 Old Gold-lt. + / 351 Coral
890 / 11	729 Old Gold-med. + / 350 Coral-med.
104 / 373	210 Lavender-med. + / 3045 Yellow Beige-dk.
19 / 9	347 Salmon-vy. dk. + / 3712 Salmon-med.
99 / 42	552 Violet-dk. + / 309 Rose-deep
27 / 8	899 Rose-med. + / 761 Salmon-lt.
9 / 13	3712 Salmon-med. + / 349 Coral-dk.
264 / 266	772 Pine Green-lt. + / 3347 Yellow Green-med.
257 / 246	3346 Hunter Green + / 895 Christmas Green-dk.
397 / 8581	3072 Beaver Gray-vy. lt. + / 647 Beaver Gray-med.
876 / 879	502 Blue Green + / 500 Blue Green-vy. dk.
22 / 99	816 Garnet + / 552 Violet-dk.
307 / 326	977 Golden Brown-lt. + / 720 Orange Spice-dk.
326 / 19	720 Orange Spice-dk. + / 347 Salmon-vy. dk.

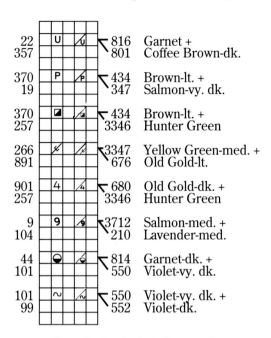

22 / 357	816 Garnet + / 801 Coffee Brown-dk.
370 / 19	434 Brown-lt. + / 347 Salmon-vy. dk.
370 / 257	434 Brown-lt. + / 3346 Hunter Green
266 / 891	3347 Yellow Green-med. + / 676 Old Gold-lt.
901 / 257	680 Old Gold-dk. + / 3346 Hunter Green
9 / 104	3712 Salmon-med. + / 210 Lavender-med.
44 / 101	814 Garnet-dk. + / 550 Violet-vy. dk.
101 / 99	550 Violet-vy. dk. + / 552 Violet-dk.

Step 3: Backstitch (1 strand)

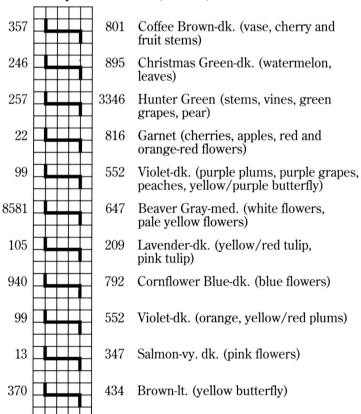

357	801 Coffee Brown-dk. (vase, cherry and fruit stems)
246	895 Christmas Green-dk. (watermelon, leaves)
257	3346 Hunter Green (stems, vines, green grapes, pear)
22	816 Garnet (cherries, apples, red and orange-red flowers)
99	552 Violet-dk. (purple plums, purple grapes, peaches, yellow/purple butterfly)
8581	647 Beaver Gray-med. (white flowers, pale yellow flowers)
105	209 Lavender-dk. (yellow/red tulip, pink tulip)
940	792 Cornflower Blue-dk. (blue flowers)
99	552 Violet-dk. (orange, yellow/red plums)
13	347 Salmon-vy. dk. (pink flowers)
370	434 Brown-lt. (yellow butterfly)

Dresser Scarf

Stitched on Vintage Linen 28 over two threads, the finished design size is 8⅝" x 8⅜". The fabric was cut 22" x 50". The design is the main floral motif of the large framed piece and is taken from the graphs on pages 88-90, 92-94, and 96-98. Measure 34" down from the short edge and 6¾" in from the left, long edge of fabric to place first stitch. Find first stitch by connecting stars on graph on page 96. Trim corners of fabric, making an oval shape. Add lace or trim as desired.

FABRICS	DESIGN SIZES
Aida 11	10⅞" x 10¾"
Aida 14	8⅝" x 8⅜"
Aida 18	6⅝" x 6½"
Hardanger 22	5½" x 5⅜"

Porcelain Jar

Stitched on Vintage Linen 28 over two threads, the finished design size is 1¾" x 2⅛". The fabric was cut 6" x 6". The design is the lower left corner floral motif of the large framed piece and is taken from the graph on page 99. Follow manufacturer's instructions to insert stitching. See page 143 for supplier.

FABRICS	DESIGN SIZES
Aida 11	2⅛" x 2¾"
Aida 14	1¾" x 2⅛"
Aida 18	1⅜" x 1⅝"
Hardanger 22	1⅛" x 1⅜"

Dresser Set

Stitched on Vintage Linen 28 over two threads, the finished design size is 1¾" x 2⅛" for the brush, and 2¾" x 2⅞" for the mirror. The fabric was cut 7" x 8" for the brush, 9" x 10" for the mirror. The design for the brush is the lower right corner floral motif taken from the graph on page 91. The design for the mirror is the grape and fruit motif spilling out of the top, left edge of the urn and is taken from the graphs on pages 93, 94, and 95. Follow manufacturer's instructions to complete the set, adding lace or trim as desired. See page 143 for supplier.

Brush

FABRICS	DESIGN SIZES
Aida 11	2⅛" x 2⅝"
Aida 14	1¾" x 2⅛"
Aida 18	1⅜" x 1⅝"
Hardanger 22	1⅛" x 1⅜"

Mirror

FABRICS	DESIGN SIZES
Aida 11	3½" x 3¾"
Aida 14	2¾" x 2⅞"
Aida 18	2⅛" x 2¼"
Hardanger 22	1¾" x 1⅞"

All of those who are
peacemakers will
plant seeds of peace
and reap a harvest
of goodness.

–James 3:18

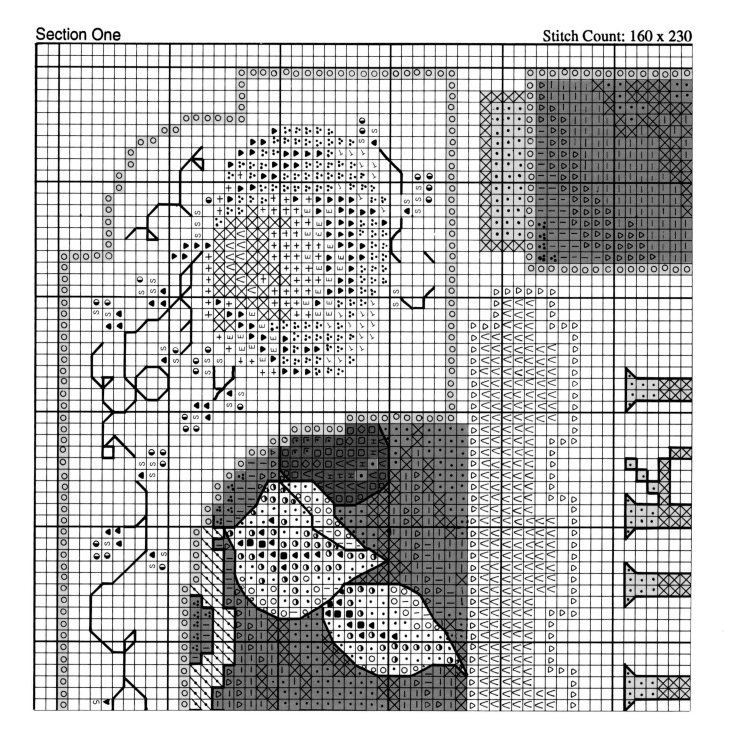

Section Two

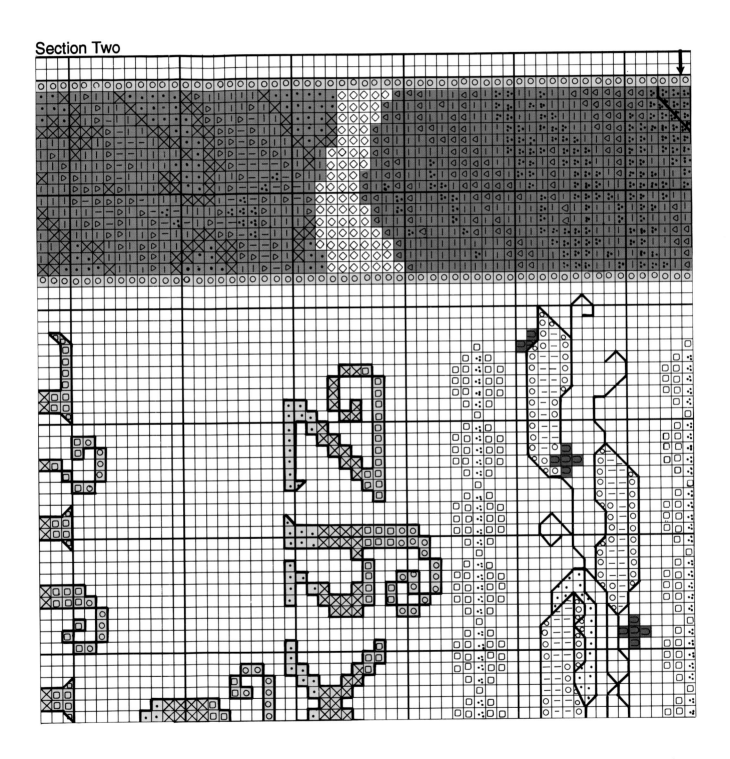

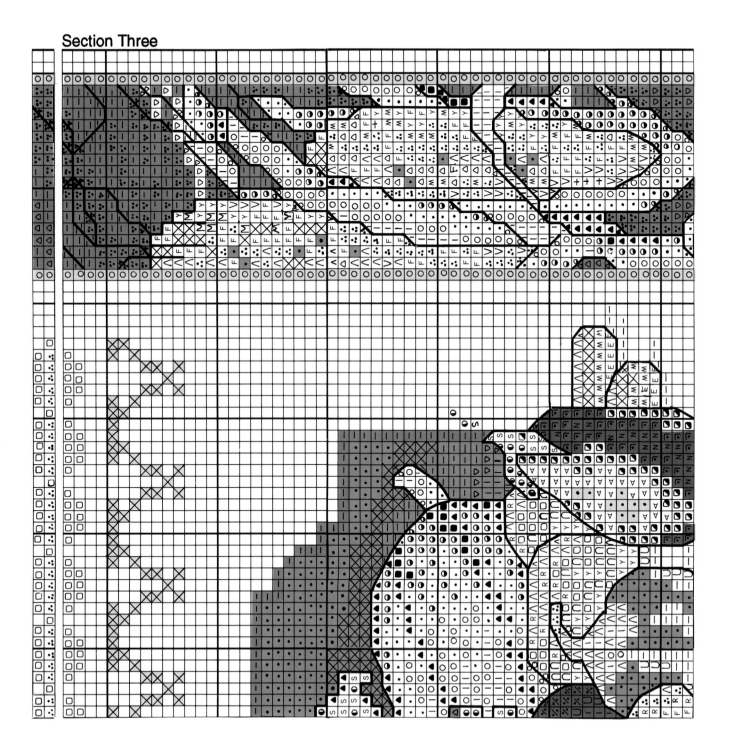

Section Four

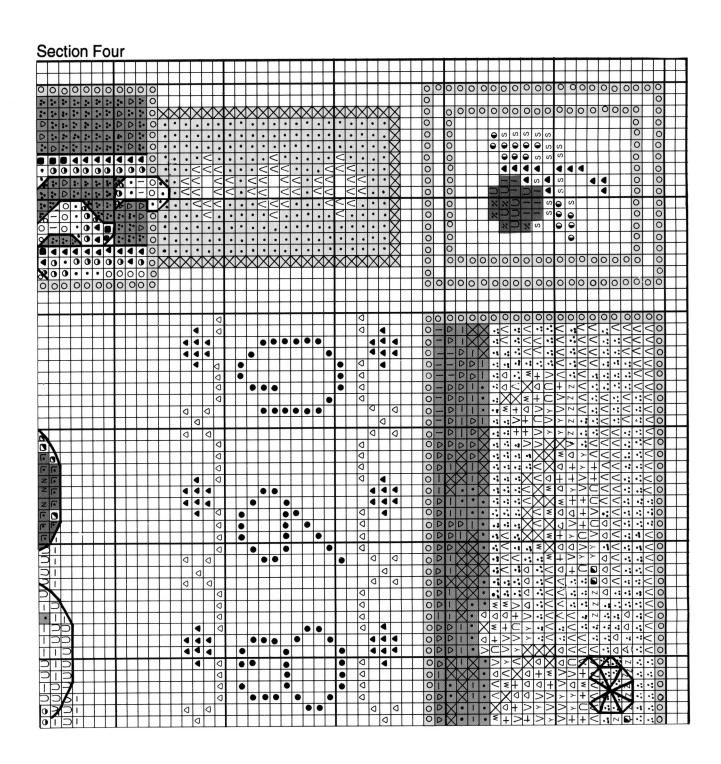

Section Five

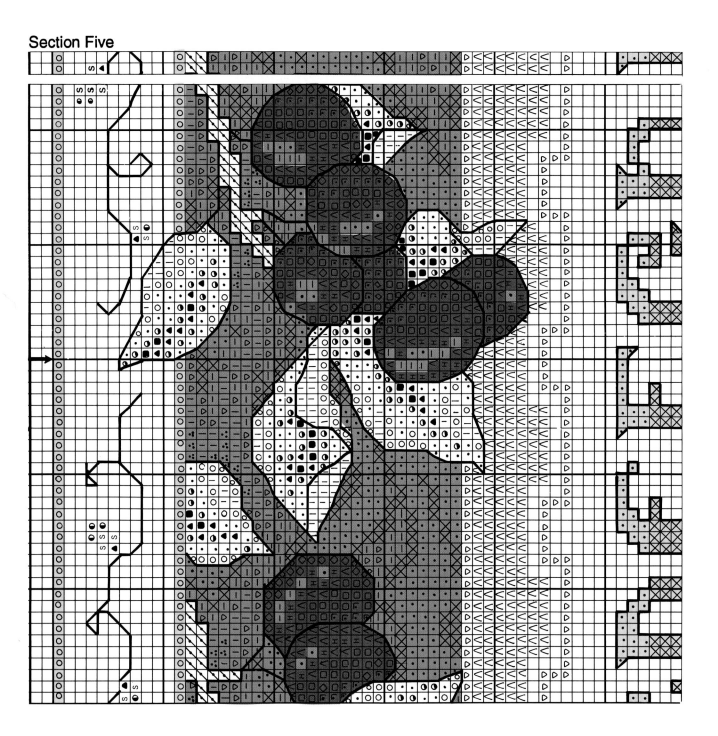

Section Six

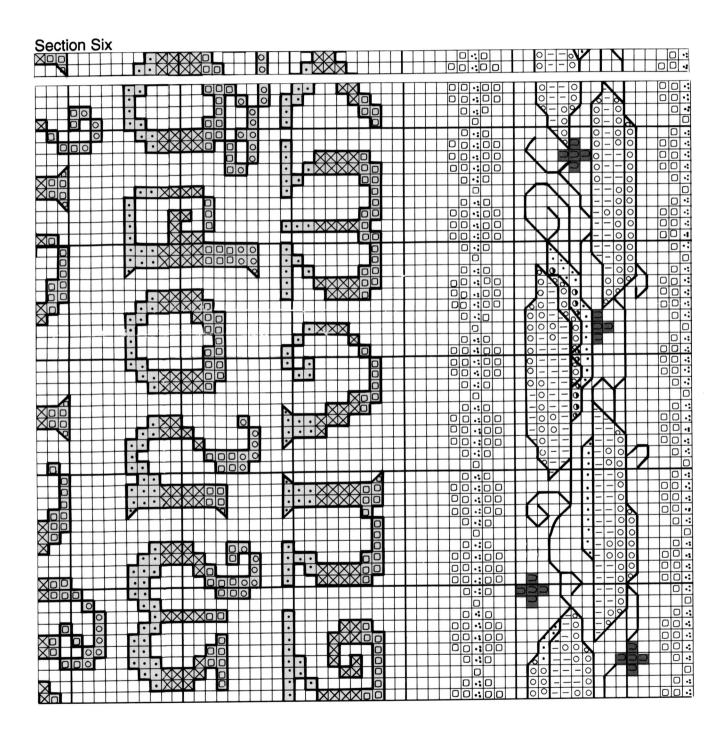

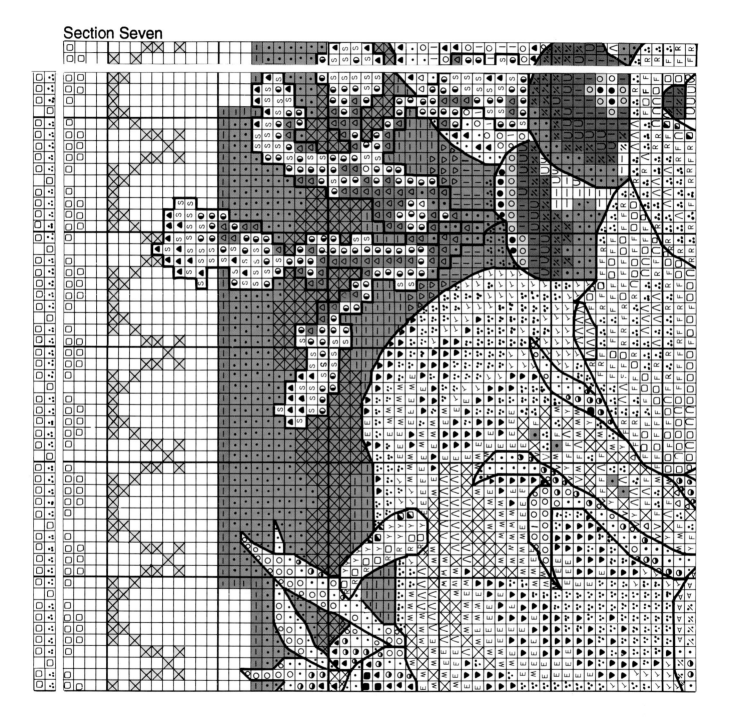

Section Eight

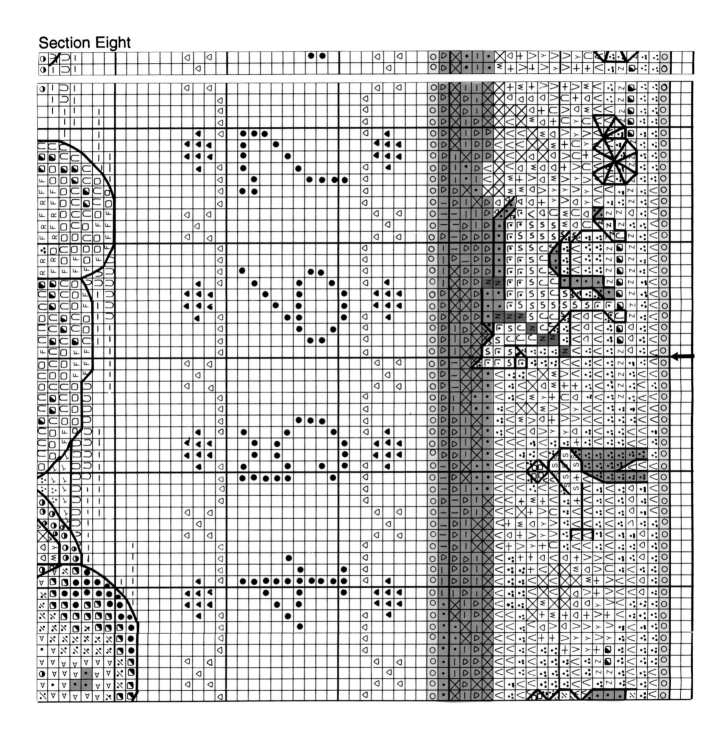

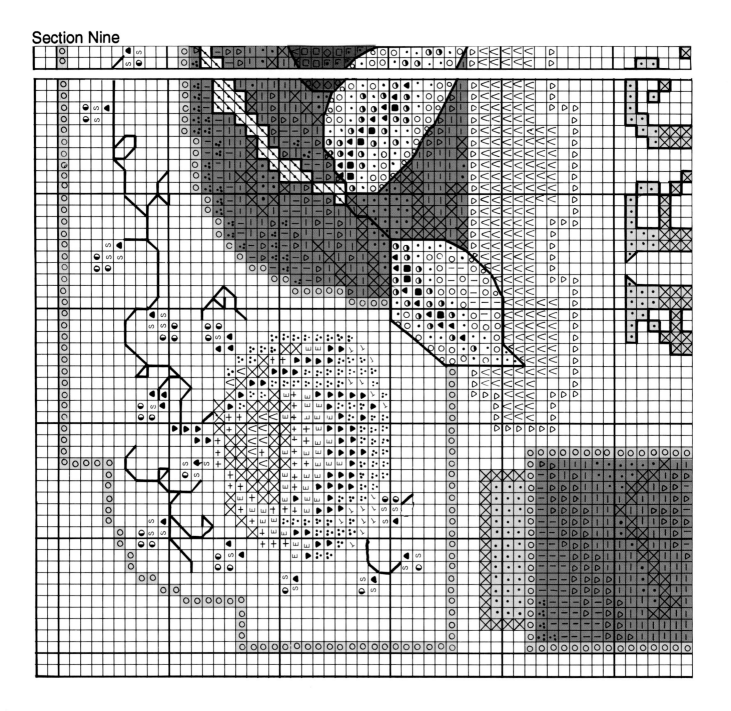

116

Section Ten

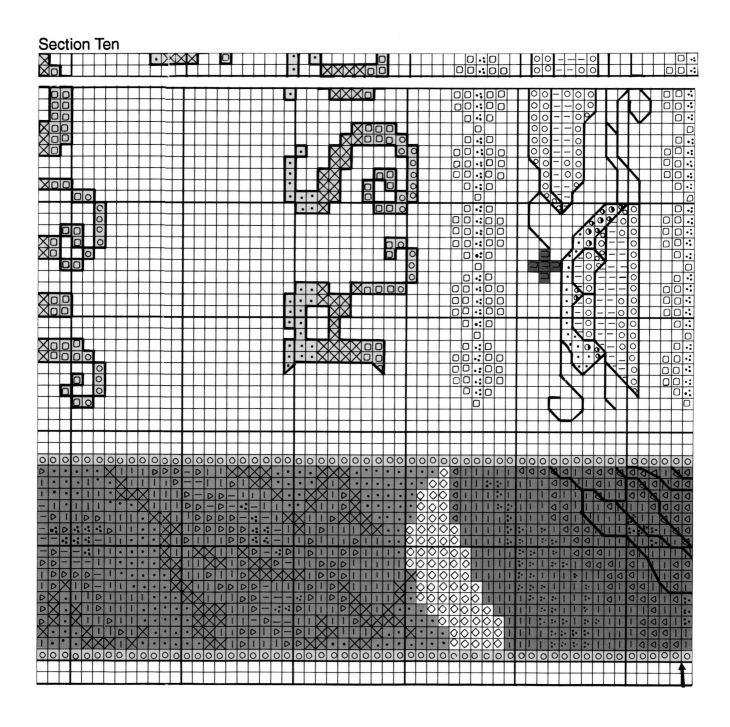

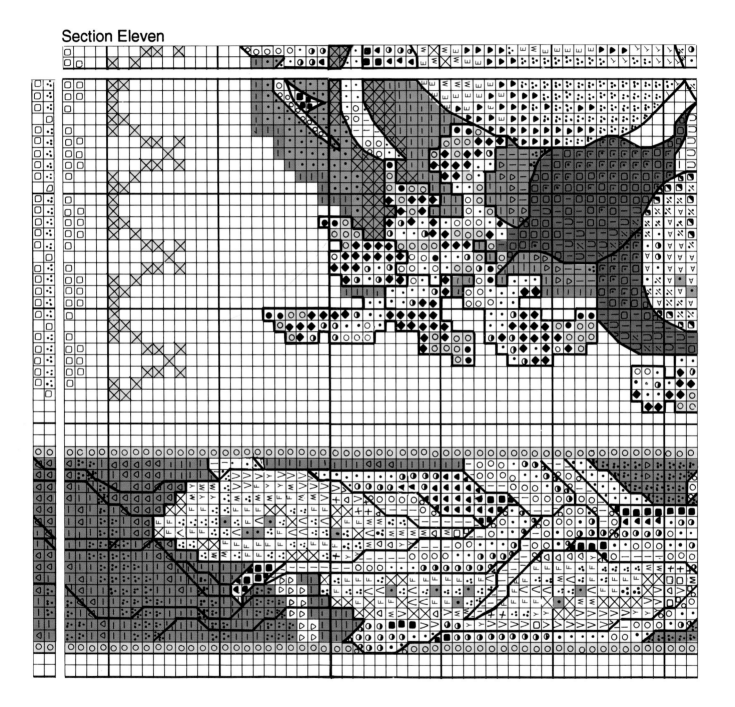

Section Twelve

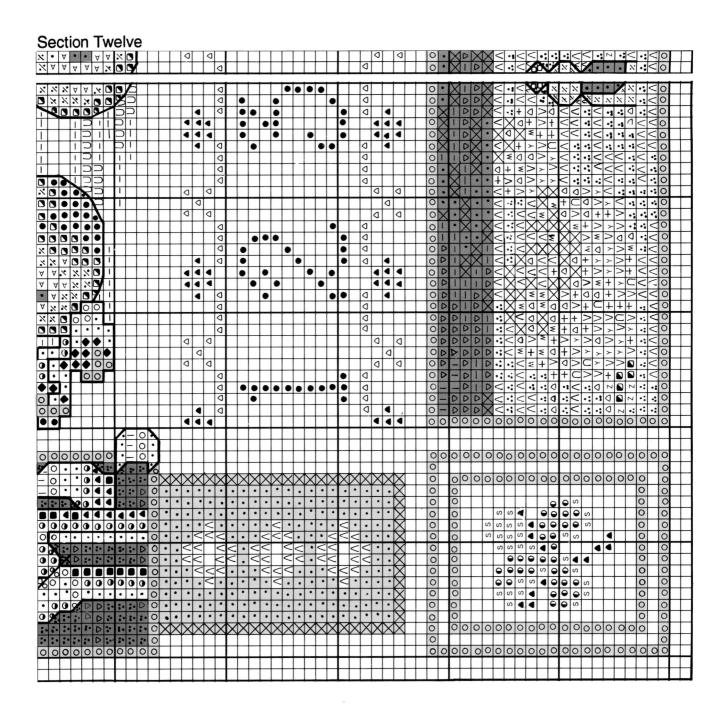

119

Harvest Sampler

Stitched on cream pastel Linen 28 over two threads, the finished design size is 11⅜" x 16⅜". The fabric was cut 18" x 23". See diagram for graph page placement. Frame piece as desired.

FABRICS	DESIGN SIZES
Aida 11	14½" x 20⅞"
Aida 14	11⅜" x 16⅜"
Aida 18	8⅞" x 12¾"
Hardanger 22	7¼" x 10½"

Stitch Count: 160 x 230

Section One (page 108)	Section Two (page 109)	Section Three (page 110)	Section Four (page 111)
Section Five (page 112)	Section Six (page 113)	Section Seven (page 114)	Section Eight (page 115)
Section Nine (page 116)	Section Ten (page 117)	Section Eleven (page 118)	Section Twelve (page 119)

Top of Design (left side label)

Diagram

Anchor		DMC (used for sample)

Step 1: Cross-stitch (2 strands)

Anchor	DMC	Color
1		White
975	3753	Antique Blue-vy. lt.
160	813	Blue-lt.
300	745	Yellow-lt. pale
891	676	Old Gold-lt.
295	726	Topaz-lt.
890	729	Old Gold-med.
370	434	Brown-lt.
307	977	Golden Brown-lt.
308	976	Golden Brown-med.
349	301	Mahogany-med.
104	210	Lavender-med.
99	552	Violet-dk.
969	3727	Antique Mauve-lt.
970	315	Antique Mauve-vy. dk.
49	3689	Mauve-lt.
66	3688	Mauve-med.

Anchor	DMC	Color
69	3687	Mauve
11	3328	Salmon-dk.
13	347	Salmon-vy. dk.
44	814	Garnet-dk.
215	320	Pistachio Green-med.
213	504	Blue Green-lt.
875	503	Blue Green-med.
876	502	Blue Green
878	501	Blue Green-dk.
264	772	Pine Green-lt.
266	3347	Yellow Green-med.
257	3346	Hunter Green
246	895	Christmas Green-dk.
862	934	Black Avocado Green
969	316	Antique Mauve-med.
363	436	Tan
216	367	Pistachio Green-dk.

120

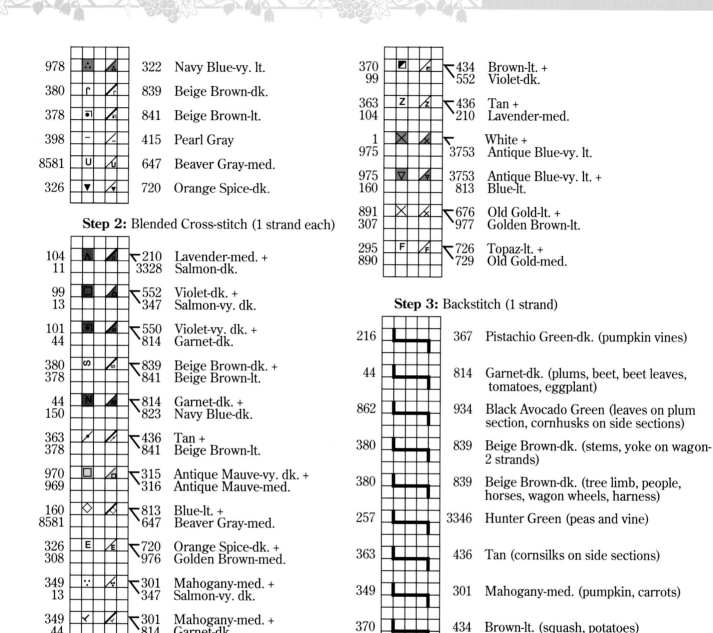

978	322	Navy Blue-vy. lt.
380	839	Beige Brown-dk.
378	841	Beige Brown-lt.
398	415	Pearl Gray
8581	647	Beaver Gray-med.
326	720	Orange Spice-dk.

Step 2: Blended Cross-stitch (1 strand each)

104 / 11	210 / 3328	Lavender-med. + Salmon-dk.
99 / 13	552 / 347	Violet-dk. + Salmon-vy. dk.
101 / 44	550 / 814	Violet-vy. dk. + Garnet-dk.
380 / 378	839 / 841	Beige Brown-dk. + Beige Brown-lt.
44 / 150	814 / 823	Garnet-dk. + Navy Blue-dk.
363 / 378	436 / 841	Tan + Beige Brown-lt.
970 / 969	315 / 316	Antique Mauve-vy. dk. + Antique Mauve-med.
160 / 8581	813 / 647	Blue-lt. + Beaver Gray-med.
326 / 308	720 / 976	Orange Spice-dk. + Golden Brown-med.
349 / 13	301 / 347	Mahogany-med. + Salmon-vy. dk.
349 / 44	301 / 814	Mahogany-med. + Garnet-dk.
13 / 44	347 / 814	Salmon-vy. dk. + Garnet-dk.
970 / 257	315 / 3346	Antique Mauve-vy. dk. + Hunter Green
264 / 266	772 / 3347	Pine Green-lt. + Yellow Green-med.
363 / 370	436 / 434	Tan + Brown-lt.

370 / 99	434 / 552	Brown-lt. + Violet-dk.
363 / 104	436 / 210	Tan + Lavender-med.
1 / 975	3753	White + Antique Blue-vy. lt.
975 / 160	3753 / 813	Antique Blue-vy. lt. + Blue-lt.
891 / 307	676 / 977	Old Gold-lt. + Golden Brown-lt.
295 / 890	726 / 729	Topaz-lt. + Old Gold-med.

Step 3: Backstitch (1 strand)

216	367	Pistachio Green-dk. (pumpkin vines)
44	814	Garnet-dk. (plums, beet, beet leaves, tomatoes, eggplant)
862	934	Black Avocado Green (leaves on plum section, cornhusks on side sections)
380	839	Beige Brown-dk. (stems, yoke on wagon-2 strands)
380	839	Beige Brown-dk. (tree limb, people, horses, wagon wheels, harness)
257	3346	Hunter Green (peas and vine)
363	436	Tan (cornsilks on side sections)
349	301	Mahogany-med. (pumpkin, carrots)
370	434	Brown-lt. (squash, potatoes)
970	315	Antique Mauve-vy. dk. (turnip, onion, alphabet)
246	895	Christmas Green-dk. (watermelon, cornhusks, turnip leaves, eggplant leaves)

Earth is here so
kind, that just tickle
her with a hoe and
she laughs with
a harvest.

–*Douglas Jerrold*

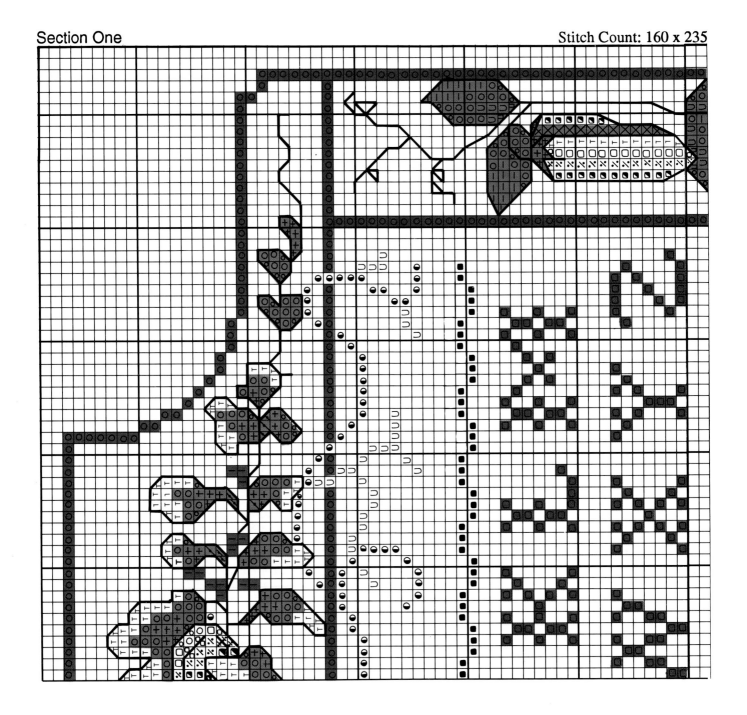

Section Two

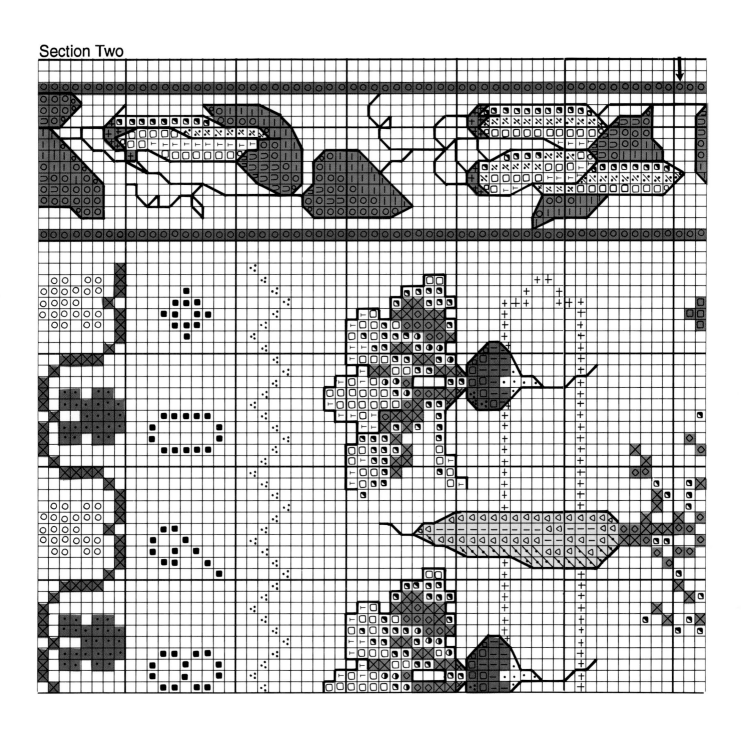

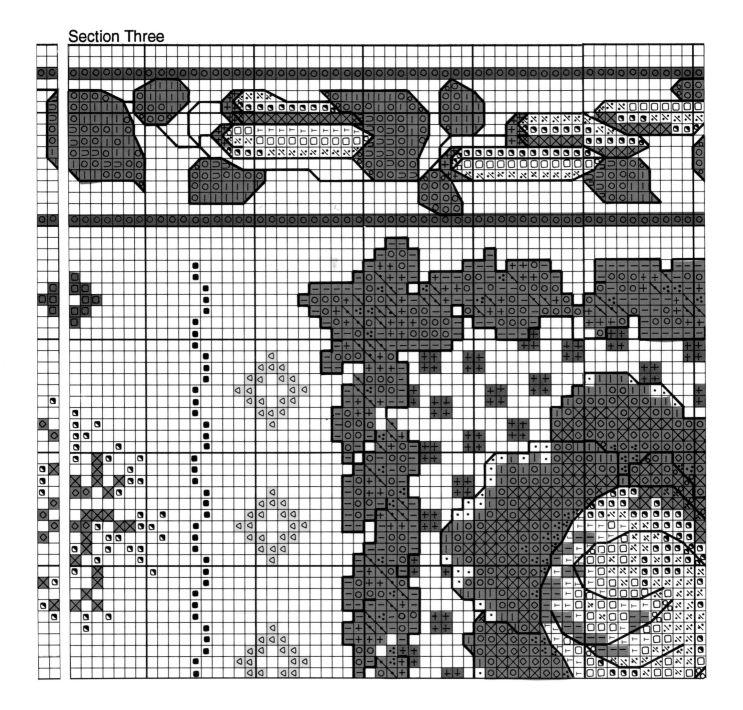

Section Four

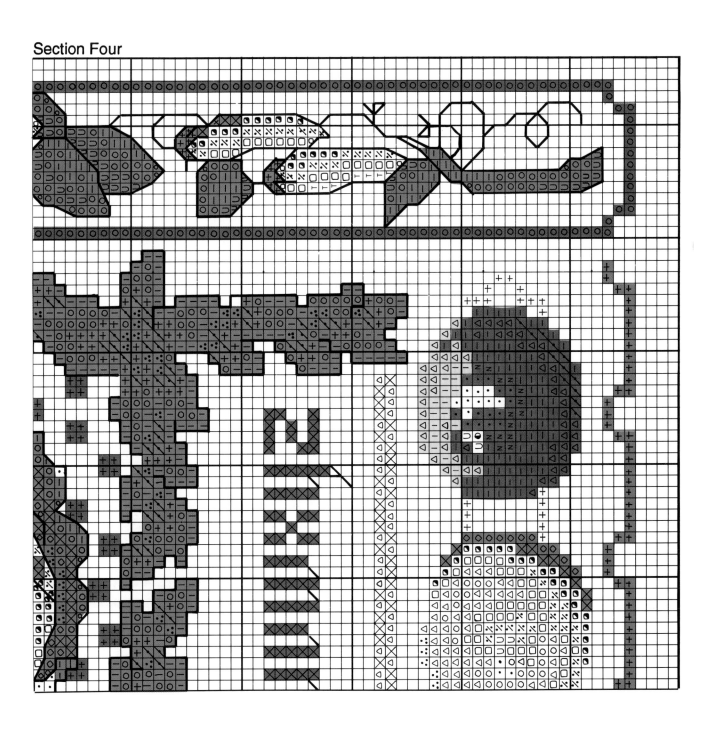

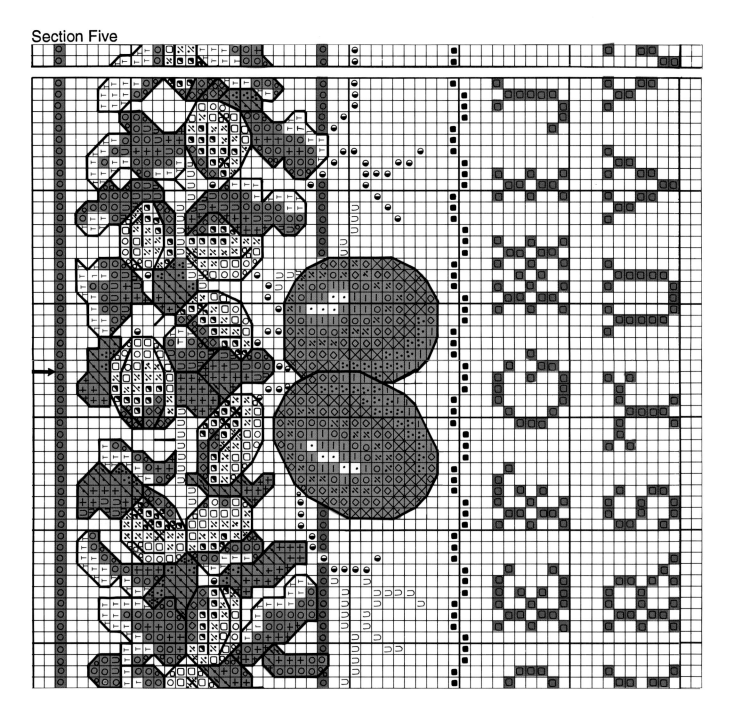

Section Six

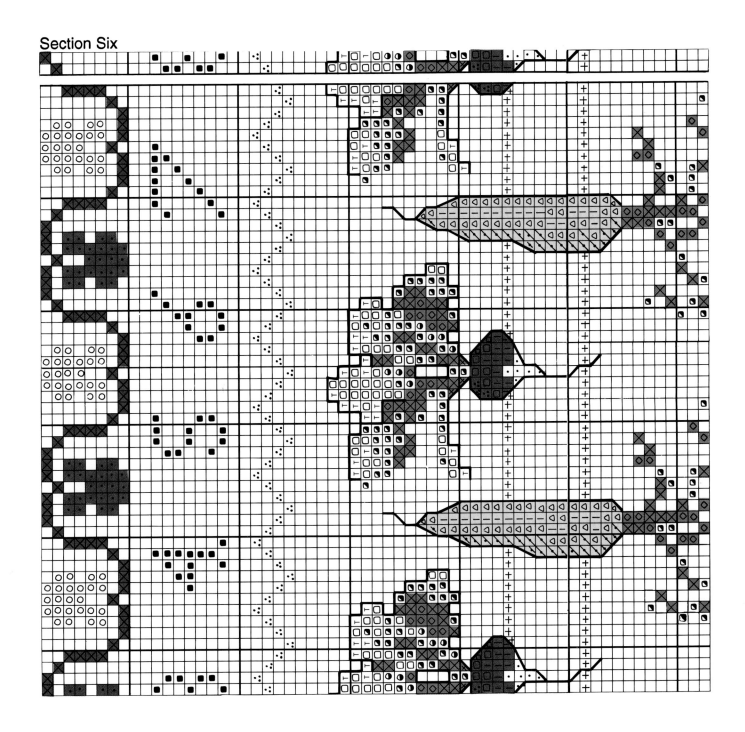

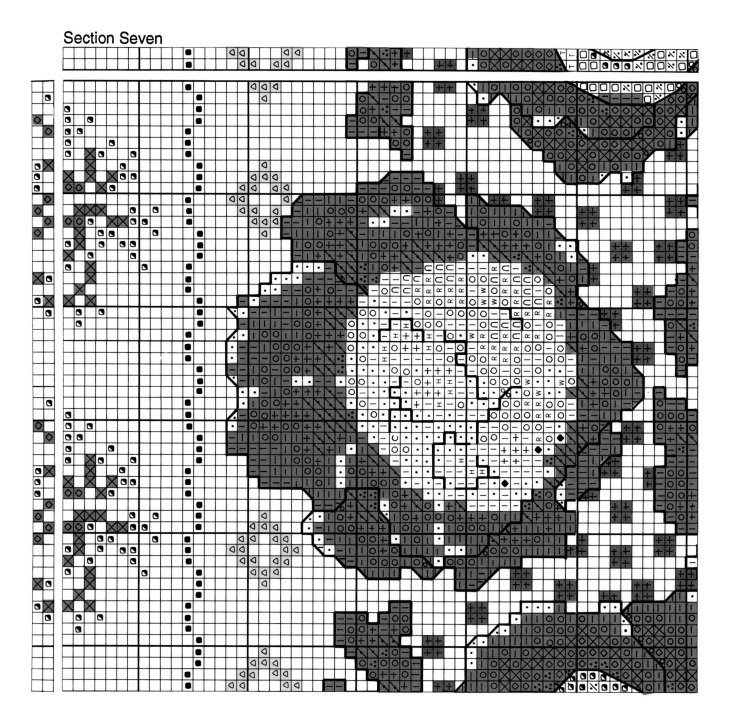

Section Eight

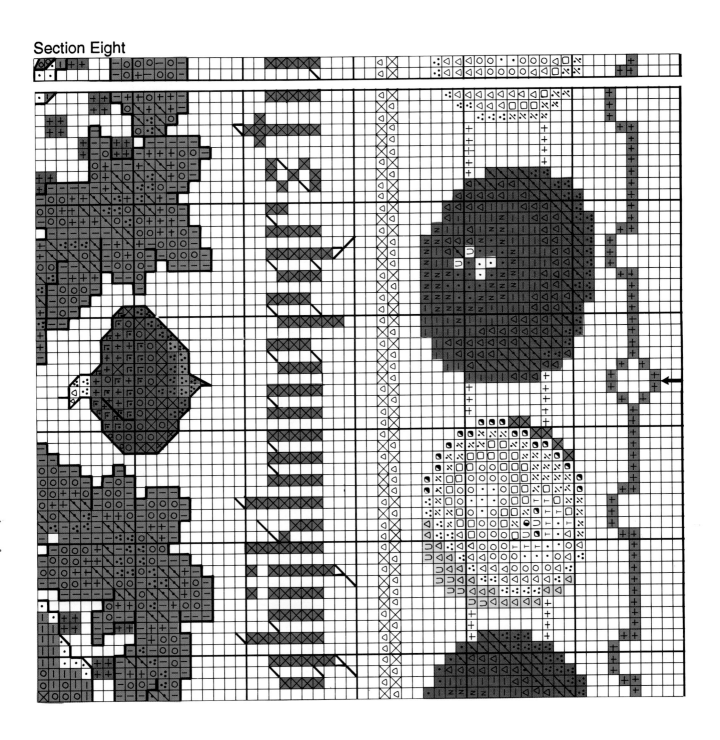

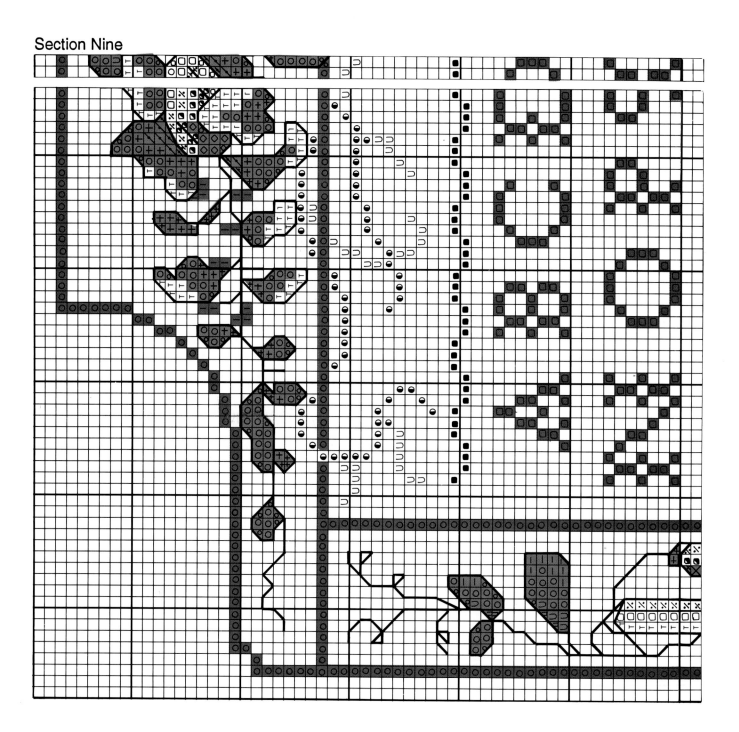

132

Section Ten

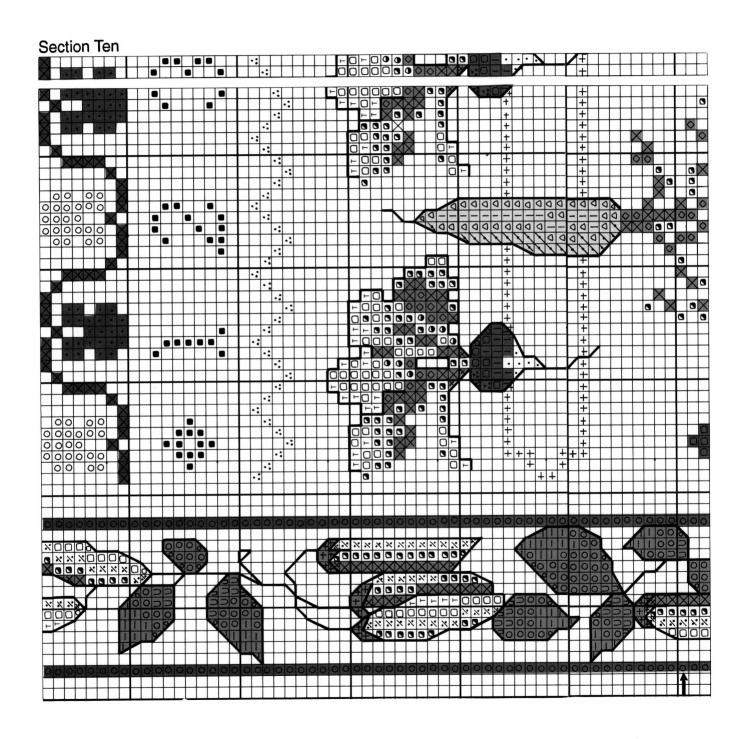

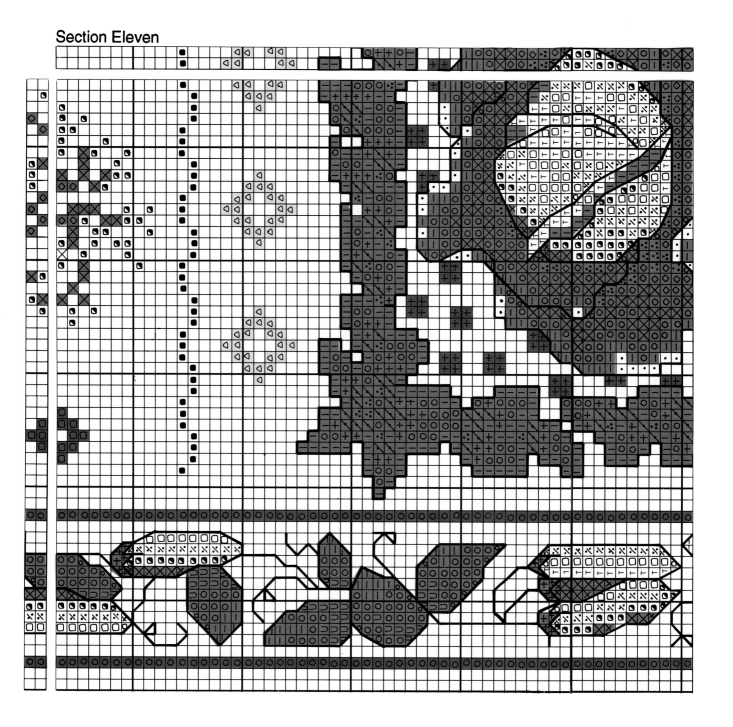

Section Twelve

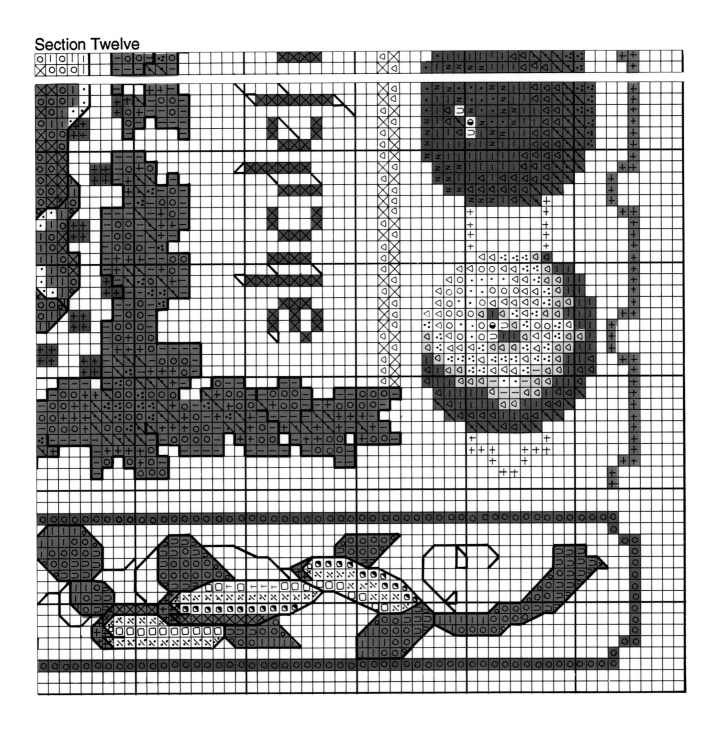

Nature's Bounty

Stitched on platinum Dublin Linen 25 over two threads, the finished design size is $12\frac{3}{4}$" x $18\frac{5}{8}$". The fabric was cut 19" x 25". See diagram below for graph page placement. Frame piece as desired.

FABRICS	DESIGN SIZES
Aida 11	$14\frac{1}{2}$" x $21\frac{1}{8}$"
Aida 14	$11\frac{3}{8}$" x $16\frac{5}{8}$"
Aida 18	$8\frac{7}{8}$" x $12\frac{7}{8}$"
Hardanger	$7\frac{1}{4}$" x $10\frac{5}{8}$"

Stitch Count: 160 x 235

<table>
<tr><td rowspan="3">Top of Design</td><td>Section One
(page 124)</td><td>Section Two
(page 125)</td><td>Section Three
(page 126)</td><td>Section Four
(page 127)</td></tr>
<tr><td>Section Five
(page 128)</td><td>Section Six
(page 129)</td><td>Section Seven
(page 130)</td><td>Section Eight
(page 131)</td></tr>
<tr><td>Section Nine
(page 132)</td><td>Section Ten
(page 133)</td><td>Section Eleven
(page 134)</td><td>Section Twelve
(page 135)</td></tr>
</table>

Diagram

Anchor   **DMC (used for sample)**

Step 1: Cross-stitch (2 strands)

Anchor			DMC	Color
1	·	⁄·		White
300	O	⁄o	745	Yellow-lt. pale
891	△	⁄△	676	Old Gold-lt.
890	∴		729	Old Gold-med.
373	✕		3045	Yellow Beige-dk.
347	I		402	Mahogany-vy. lt.
324	△	⁄△	922	Copper-lt.
9	▪		760	Salmon
11	U		3328	Salmon-dk.
11	▬		350	Coral-med.
19	▲		817	Coral Red-vy. dk.
22	◢		816	Garnet
44	∴	⁄▪	814	Garnet-dk.
893	+	⁄	224	Shell Pink-lt.
896	⊙	⁄o	3722	Shell Pink
897	✕	⁄	221	Shell Pink-vy. dk.
66	▪	⁄	3688	Mauve-med.
69	▣	⁄	3687	Mauve

Anchor			DMC	Color
900	+	⁄+	648	Beaver Gray-lt.
8581	◆		647	Beaver Gray-med.
401	W		844	Beaver Gray-ultra dk.
375	U	⁄U	420	Hazel Nut Brown-dk.
371	◑	⁄o	433	Brown-med.
104	▬	⁄	210	Lavender-med.
118	⊙		340	Blue Violet-med.
119	■		3746	Blue Violet-dk.
101	✕	⁄✕	327	Antique Violet-vy. dk.
213	▪	⁄▬	504	Blue Green-lt.
216	+	⁄+	367	Pistachio Green-dk.
214	⊙	⁄o	368	Pistachio Green-lt.
879	∴	⁄▪	500	Blue Green-vy. dk.
264	□	⁄□	472	Avocado Green-ultra lt.
264	T	⁄T	772	Pine Green-lt.
266	◪	⁄◪	3347	Yellow Green-med.
257	✕	⁄✕	3346	Hunter Green
246	⊖		895	Christmas Green-dk.

Step 2: Blended Cross-stitch (1 strand each)

257 / 246	3346 / 895	Hunter Green + Christmas Green-dk.
897 / 324	221 / 922	Shell Pink-vy. dk. + Copper-lt.
44 / 101	814 / 327	Garnet-dk. + Antique Violet-vy. dk.
119 / 11	3746 / 3328	Blue Violet-dk. + Salmon-dk.
119 / 9	3746 / 760	Blue Violet-dk. + Salmon
1 / 213	White / 504	White + Blue Green-lt.
216 / 879	367 / 500	Pistachio Green-dk. + Blue Green-vy. dk.
264 / 266	472 / 3347	Avocado Green-ultra lt. + Yellow Green-med.
214 / 216	368 / 367	Pistachio Green-lt. + Pistachio Green-dk.
104 / 900	210 / 648	Lavender-med. + Beaver Gray-lt.
900 / 1	648 / White	Beaver Gray-lt. + White
264 / 8581	472 / 647	Avocado Green-ultra lt. + Beaver Gray-med.
266 / 8581	3347 / 647	Yellow Green-med. + Beaver Gray-med.
893 / 896	224 / 3722	Shell Pink-lt. + Shell Pink
11 / 9	350 / 760	Coral-med. + Salmon

Step 3: Backstitch (1 strand)

216	367	Pistachio Green-dk. (gooseberries and leaves on top section, radish leaves, cauliflower leaves, leaves around cabbage, vine and leaves)
264	772	Pine Green-lt. (inside gooseberries)
375	420	Hazel Nut Brown-dk. (gooseberry vine)
101	327	Antique Violet-vy. dk. (plums)
896	3722	Shell Pink (radishes)
897	221	Shell Pink-vy. dk. (carrots, lowercase lettering)
401	844	Beaver Gray-ultra dk. (inside cauliflower)
257	3346	Hunter Green (cabbage and leaves)
44	814	Garnet-dk. (red onion)
246	895	Christmas Green-dk. (peas)

138

Wreath

Stitched on Perforated Plastic over one mesh, the finished design size is 2½" x 2⅛" for lettuce, 2⅝" x 2¾" for cauliflower, 2⅝" x 2⅛" for cabbage, 1½" x 2¾" for carrot, 1⅜" x 1¾" for radish, 1⅛" x 1⅛" for the first apple (see bottom row of sampler on page 123), 1¼" x 1⅛" for the third apple, 1⅜" x 1⅛" for the fourth apple. The plastic was cut 6" x 6" for each design. Place stitched design pieces as desired on purchased wreath. The fruit and vegetable designs are taken from the graphs on pages 124-135.

Recipe Box

Stitched on platinum Belfast Linen 32 over two threads, the finished design size is 9½" x 2". The fabric was cut 16" x 8". The design is the plum garland at the top of the sampler and is taken from the graphs on pages 124, 128, and 132. Paint box if desired, then follow manufacturer's instructions for inserting stitching. See page 143 for supplier.

FABRICS	DESIGN SIZES
Aida 11	13⅞" x 3"
Aida 14	10⅞" x 2⅜"
Aida 18	8½" x 1⅞"
Hardanger 22	6⅞" x 1½"

CROSS-STITCH TIPS

FABRICS: Counted cross-stitch is usually worked on even-weave fabric. These fabrics are manufactured specifically for counted-thread embroidery and are woven with the same number of vertical as horizontal threads per inch. Because the number of threads in the fabric is equal in each direction, each stitch will be square. It is the number of threads per inch in even-weave fabrics that determines the size of a finished design.

WASTE CANVAS: Waste Canvas is a loosely woven fabric used as a guide for cross-stitching on fabrics other than even-weaves. Cut the waste canvas 1" larger on all sides than the finished design size. Baste it to the fabric to be stitched. Complete the stitching. Then, dampen the stitched area with cold water. Pull out the waste canvas threads one at a time with tweezers. It is easier to pull all the threads running in one direction first, then pull out the opposite threads. Allow the stitching to dry. Place face down on a towel and iron.

PREPARING FABRIC: Cut even-weave fabric at least 3" larger on all sides than the design size. A 3" margin is the minimum amount of space that allows for comfortably working the edges of the design. To prevent fraying, whipstitch or machine-zigzag raw fabric edges.

NEEDLES: Needles should slip easily through the holes in the fabric but not pierce the threads. Use a blunt tapestry needle, size 24 or 26. Never leave the needle in the design area of your work. It can leave rust or a permanent impression on the fabric.

FLOSS: Cut the floss into 18" lengths. Run the floss over a damp sponge to straighten. Separate all six strands and use the number of strands called for in the code.

CENTERING THE DESIGN: Fold the fabric in half horizontally, then vertically. Place a pin in the fold point to mark the center. Locate the center of the design on the graph by following the vertical and horizontal arrows on the top, bottom, and sides of the graph. Begin stitching all designs at the center points of the graph and the fabric.

GRAPHS: Each symbol, or colored symbol, represents a different floss color. Make one stitch for each symbol, referring to the code to verify which stitch to use. Use the small arrows on the top, bottom, and sides of the graph to find the center. When a graph is continued, the two rows on the bottom or side of the graph on the previous page are repeated, separated by a small space, indicating where to connect them. The stitch count is printed with each graph, listing first the width, then the length of the design.

CODES: The code indicates the brand of floss used to stitch the model and all floss numbers and color names are cross-referenced between Anchor and DMC brands. The steps in the code identify the stitch to be used and the number of floss strands for that stitch. The symbols match the graph, and give the color number for the thread. A symbol under a diagonal line indicates a half-cross-stitch. Blended threads are represented on the code and graph with a single symbol, but both color names are listed.

SECURING THE FLOSS: Insert your needle up from the underside of the fabric at your starting point. Hold 1" of thread behind the fabric and stitch over it, securing it with the first few stitches. To finish the thread, run under four or more stitches on the back of the design. Never knot floss unless working on clothing. Another method of securing floss is the waste knot. Knot your floss and insert your needle from the right side of the fabric about 1" inside the design area. Work several stitches over the thread to secure. Cut off the knot later.

STITCHING: For a smooth cross-stitch, use the "push-and-pull" method. Start by bringing the needle straight up from wrong side of fabric, pulling floss completely through to right side with the exception of the first stitch. Re-insert needle and bring it back straight down, pulling needle and floss completely through to back of fabric. Keep floss flat but do not pull tight. Consistent tension throughout ensures even stitches. Make one stitch for every symbol on the chart. To stitch in rows, work from left to right and then back. Half-crosses are used to make a rounded shape. Make the longer stitch in the direction of the slanted line.

CARRYING FLOSS: To carry floss, weave floss under the previously worked stitches on the back. Do not carry thread across any fabric that is not or will not be stitched. Loose threads, especially dark ones, will show through the fabric.

CLEANING COMPLETED WORK: When stitching is complete, soak it in cold water with a mild soap for 5–10 minutes; rinse. Roll in a towel to remove excess water. Do not wring. Place work face down on a dry towel and iron on a warm setting until dry.

STITCHES

CROSS-STITCH: Make one cross-stitch for each symbol on chart. Bring needle up at A, down at B, up at C, down at D. For rows, stitch across fabric

from left to right to make half-crosses and then back to complete stitches. All stitches should lie in the same direction.

HALF-CROSS-STITCH: The stitch actually fits three-fourths of the area. Make the longer stitch in the direction of the slanted line on the graph. Bring needle and thread up at A, down at B, up at C, and down at D.

BACKSTITCH: Working from right to left with one strand of floss (unless designated otherwise on code), bring needle and thread up at A, down at B, and up again at C. Go back down at A and continue in this manner. NOTE: Complete all cross-stitching before working backstitches or other accent stitches.

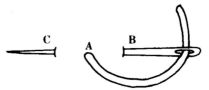

FRENCH KNOT: Bring the needle up at A, using one strand of embroidery floss. Wrap floss around needle two times. Insert needle beside A, pulling floss until it fits snugly around needle. Pull needle through to back.

142

Suppliers

Fabrics
Wichelt Imports, Inc.
Rural Route 1
Stoddard, WI 54658

Zweigart Fabrics/Joan Toggitt
2 Riverview Drive
Somerset, NJ 08873-1139

Metallic Thread
Kreinik Mfg. Co., Inc.
P.O. Box 1966
Parkersburg, WV 26102

Wood Boxes
Reed Baxter Woodcrafts Inc.
P.O. Box 2186
Eugene, OR 97402

Porcelain Jars & Dresser Set
Anne Brinkley Designs Inc.
21 Ransom Road
Newton Centre, MA 02159

Towels & Bread Cover
Charles Craft
P.O. Box 1049
Laurinburg, NC 28353

Perforated Plastic
Darice Incorporated Products
21160 Drake Road
Strongsville, OH 44136

Index

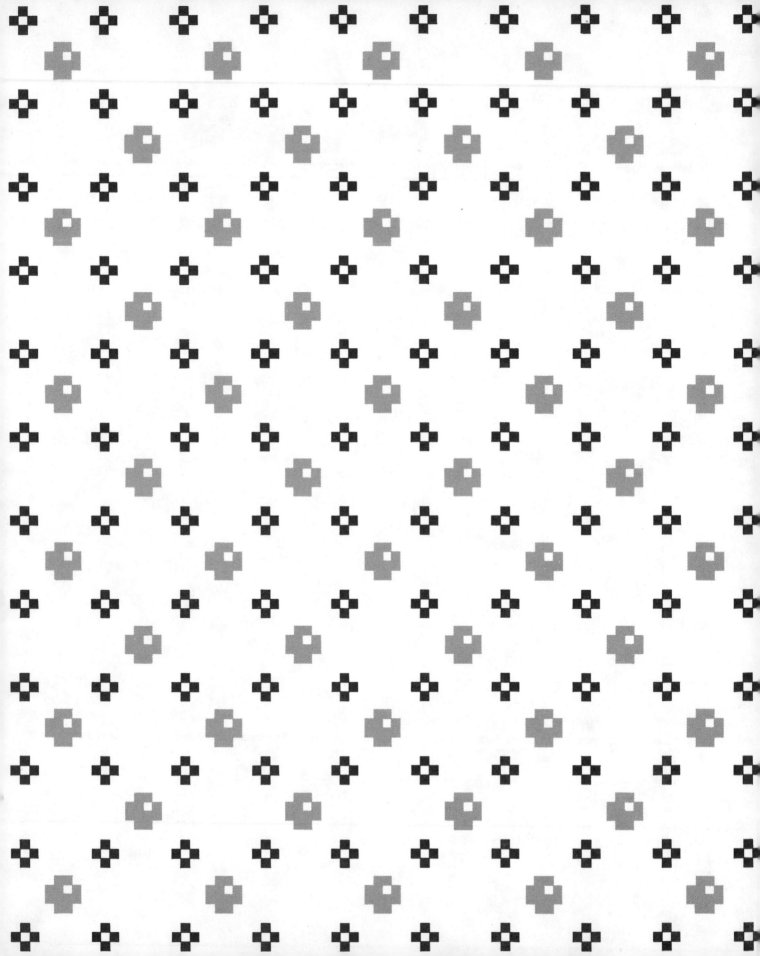